EXPOSING THE WHEEL
SPIN ON WALL STREET

Exposing the Wheel Spin on Wall Street

Ted Lux

Writers Club Press
San Jose New York Lincoln Shanghai

Exposing the Wheel Spin on Wall Street

Published by Writers Club Press
an imprint of iUniverse.com, Inc.

For information address:
iUniverse.com, Inc.
620 North 48th Street, Suite 201
Lincoln, NE 68504-3467
www.iuniverse.com

ISBN: 0-595-12319-8

Printed in the United States of America

This book is dedicated to my son Matthew who is the true joy and love in my life. It's a thanks to my parents and family members who have had to put up with me. A special thank you to Tom, for helping edit. The book reaches out to all my friends near and far.

Preface

The following pages are written with the intent of educating and providing insights into the world of investing. The book is not overly analytical, statistical or complicated. It is intended to be easy to read and follow. It's hopeful that the investment novice, the Harvard Business School graduate and the Wall Street professional can gain something from its contents and apply to his or her investment practices.

The large Wall Street firms such as Morgan Stanley Dean Witter, Merrill Lynch and Goldman Sachs & Co. employ many brilliant people. The recently departed Treasury Secretary, Robert Rubin, was in fact, prior to his role in government, a partner for many years with Goldman Sachs. The list can go on and on about qualified and well-educated people on Wall Street. When I came out of business school in the early 1980's many of my classmates, including myself, sought high paying and high profile jobs in investment banking, research and investment management. Competition was, and still is, fierce for these positions on Wall Street. I never did land one of those high profile jobs in New York where starting salaries today are in many cases in excess of $100,000 for young twenty-four year-olds coming out of business school. This of course excludes bonuses and other perks the investment houses heap on top business school grads.

After completing my MBA in 1982, I pursued my interest in Finance and worked for several organizations in the real estate financing industry, including Travelers Insurance Company and CB Commercial (now known as CB Richard Ellis). Finally, in the mid 1990's for my own sanity and financial well being I needed to do something else. It wasn't that I didn't know the loan business. It was just that there were so few loans being made and my luck seemed to be drying up as interest rates escalated through most of 1994. Later that fall, I did get a job with Dean Witter Reynolds & Co. in Beverly Hills, California (now known as Morgan Stanley Dean Witter through the merger of the two firms a few years ago). After a few months of study and licensing, I went to work as an Account Executive. In a previous era this was known as a stockbroker. I felt I had "finally arrived," but that feeling was short lived and only lasted a couple of months. During my brief tenure there, I did meet some very good, hard working and intelligent people. Some have remained close friends since my departure in late 1997.

What drew me to pursue a career in investments was that I have always believed in investing and saving for one's future. I guess it has something to do with my family and my "good Midwestern values" we hear of so often. Therefore, my attraction to pursue and obtain an MBA and a career in the investment world. I thought I could do a lot of good for other people by giving sound investment advice and direction and yet make a good living following such practices. As time went by I became very disillusioned with life from within the firm. I was failing miserably as a stockbroker in terms of attracting capital to the firm and generating commissions. I guess if I was still working for a Wall Street firm and doing all the things I was supposed to do (from the firm's point of view) this book would never have been written. You see I am now an outsider and have nothing to gain or lose by the contents of this book. I don't care if I piss off a few people nor do I care about the scathing commentary I make about an industry I'm convinced exists and prospers by fleecing the American public.

About a decade ago I read something Ross Perot was quoted in saying which has stuck with me for many years. Now Ross Perot has said a lot of things over the years and I do find him entertaining and humorous. But what he said about Wall Street was that the investment houses "are paying a bunch of twenty- eight year old kids with MBA's $400,000 a year and they don't know what they're doing." While I was employed as an Account Executive I put my MBA to good use and found out how true this comment was. This book in essence is here to provide proof to Mr. Perot's quotation and to shed additional light on the fact that even those that know what they're doing with your money on Wall Street take advantage of you anyway.

Isaac Newton, the great seventeenth century English scientist, who brought forth the theories of gravitational forces in his book, *Philosophiae Naturalis Principia Mathematica,* in 1687, was just forty-five years old at the time. Albert Einstein, in 1915, developed his theory of relativity (e = mc^2) when he was only thirty-six years old. Now I don't claim to have as great a mind as either of these two thinkers (and those that know me far from it) but being forty-one and having spent the last fifteen or so years in the financial industry I feel compelled to sing out. I hope you enjoy the pages ahead and find them beneficial.

PART 1

What to Avoid Doing

In the investment market the return you receive is made up of two parts. First, is the current yield or dividends one receives from one's investment. Dividends are usually paid each quarter by corporations to their shareholders. Mutual fund owners however, receive their dividends annually and mostly towards year-end. Secondly, return is made up of capital appreciation on dollars invested over the length of time you own the investment. Over the years, capital appreciation has contributed a much higher percentage of your total return than the dividends you receive on a periodic basis.

Many studies have shown that the return in the stock market in the twentieth century has provided a 10% to 11% average annualized return, depending on the index for evaluation and when the study was conducted. For example, the reporting agency Ibbotson, notes at its web site that from 1929—1998 the market provided an 11% annualized return. Of that return, approximately 70% have come to us through capital appreciation and the remaining 30% from the receipt of dividends. These components have shifted in relative weight over time. In some years, the receipt of dividends provide a much greater return than capital or market appreciation. During the 1973—1974 recession for example, the market tumbled about 47% in those two years, and any return you did have was the result of dividends received. Therefore, the ratio of return was 0% from appreciation and 100% from dividends. However, over the twentieth century the average or norm is about 70/30.

During the last one hundred years this country faced the market crash in 1929 and the ensuing depression of the 1930's. It also faced the deep recession in 1973—1974. The markets performed very poorly during these periods and therefore historical performance is lower over a much longer time frame (an 11% return from 1929 is a lot less than an 18% return or so over the last ten years). I don't think we as investors can be duped into thinking that the market can continue to outperform its longer-term rate of return indefinitely. History has a way of repeating itself.

Wealth is created in part by achieving a high compounded rate of return. If you took $10,000 in 1990 and invested in the market and achieved the historical return of 11% per annum the investment would be worth approximately $28,400 in 2000. That's not bad and nothing to sneeze at. But, if we compare that to the ten-year return of 18.21%, which the Standard and Poors 500 index achieved through December 1999, (according to figures published by Standard & Poors) the $10,000 invested in 1990 would be worth approximately $53,275. Clearly, with the low inflation rate we face today, investors in the general market, have outperformed earlier generations of aunts, uncles and grandfathers. Indeed, the last decade has been exceptional to all of us invested in the market.

Now let's see by example what would happen in the next ten years to your $10,000 should we compare the returns from above. By 2010, the value of your original investment in 1990 would grow to about $80,600 assuming an 11% annual return. In comparison, the same $10,000 invested in 1990 would be worth an amazing $283,800 by 2010 assuming the rate of return of 18.21% for the Standard & Poors 500 index hold true for another ten years. There is a huge difference between $80,600 and $283,800. I'd rather have the additional $203,200 in my pocket.

The above comments illustrate the two keys to successful investing. First, the compounded annualized rate of return you achieve (in our example above either 11% or 18.21%) makes a huge difference in wealth creation. Second, and just as important is the length of time you achieve the return. We see in the above example that from the years 2000 to 2010 your wealth grows from $28,400 to $80,600 at 11% and from $53,275 to $283,800 at 18.21%. The amount of time you have your money invested and at work for you is vital to your wealth creation. Little else matters in the investment world towards wealth creation outside of these two principles. The tough part is how to do it. What pitfalls should you, the investor, avoid and what actions can you take to help maximize your return and create wealth?

The rest of this book seeks to answer some of these questions for you.

Wealth can be created in a number of ways that I know of:

You can marry into it or divorce it;

You can create or invent a product or service that nobody has and everybody wants and sell it (Thomas Edison, Henry Ford & Bill Gates);

You can get lucky and hit the lottery, or;

You can invest and put your hard-earned capital into appreciable assets like stocks or real estate.

I'll be dealing with the last item in the pages that follow.

Now let's take a closer look at how to invest and what to avoid so that you can retire comfortably and work on improving your golf game.

Two of the most widely used indices for judging US stock performance is the Standard & Poors 500 index and the Dow Jones Industrial Average. Now these indexes are not descended to us from the heavens above. They are in fact man made, picked by humans and changing. The stocks that comprise each index have changed significantly throughout the years and continue to do so. In fact, from January 1, 1999 through October 31, 1999, twenty-nine stocks have been replaced in the S & P 500. The Dow has had similar replacements over the years and Home Depot, Intel, Microsoft and SBC Communications replaced most recently Chevron, Goodyear, Sears and Union Carbide. Prior to these late 1999 changes, about two years ago, the Dow went through a similar amendment whereby Bethlehem Steel, Texaco, Westinghouse and Woolworth were dropped in favor of Hewlett-Packard, Johnson & Johnson, Travelers (now Citigroup) and Wal-Mart. Most of these changes are due to the evolving nature of our economy as it has changed over the last century from an agricultural to smokestack society and now into a service and technological based one. A proper cross section of our economy is attempted to comprise each index.

If we look at Charts 1, 2 and 3, we can see how closely the two indexes have performed over time. Although slight deviation can be found, it is astounding how closely the two indexes move in tandem over time as represented in the graph from 1950 to present. The second chart depicts the total return of both the S & P 500 and the Dow for the last five years through January 3, 2000 as reported by Bloomberg. Again, it is uncanny how close the returns have been. Bloomberg reports these total returns to be 197.28% for the Dow Jones Average and 218.93% for the S & P 500 for this five-year period. The returns are remarkably equivalent!

CHART 1

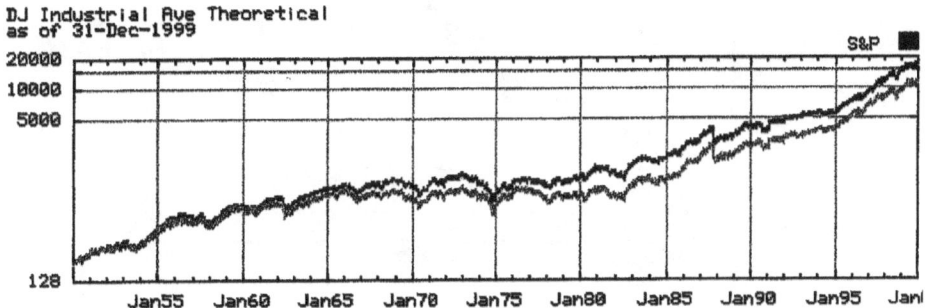

DJ Industrial Ave Theoretical
as of 31-Dec-1999

CHART 2

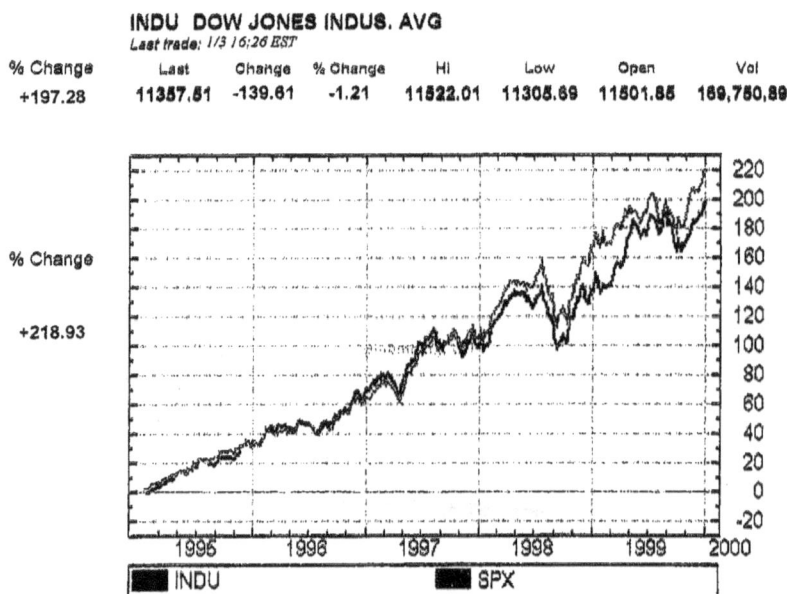

As mentioned before, over the last ten years through December 1999, the return of the S & P 500 has been reported at 18.21% on an annualized basis. Coincidentally, the Dow Jones Industrial Average returned 18.62% during a comparable time period (according to Dow Jones & Co.,). Again, upon inspection of the third chart below it shows a remarkable similarity in returns over the last ten years of the two important indexes.

CHART 3

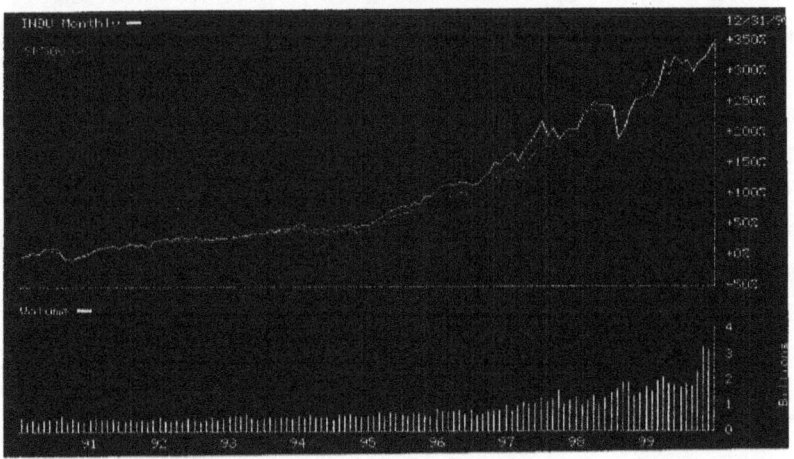

Source: Reprinted, by permission of BigCharts.com

According to information obtained at motleyfool.com, the S & P 500 and the Dow Jones Industrial Average produced the exact same return of 12.67% for the thirty-year period from 1969—1998. Again remarkable! It's quite apparent that if you owned the stocks underlying the Dow Jones Industrial Average, which total thirty companies, you would have received the equivalent return of the Standard and Poors 500, which totals quite a bit more. It is impractical to own 500 companies outright unless you have a compulsive-neurotic disorder. Thirty stocks produce the same returns any ways. (Please see Appendix A for a current listing of the stocks comprising the Dow Jones Industrial Average). The important lesson this teaches us is you don't need to own a lot of stocks to achieve market returns. The quantity of stocks owned does not help your returns whatsoever.

Lets' digress for a moment because this brings up the exciting subject of, diversification, in the investment world. Diversification means the idea of not putting all your eggs into one basket—a phrase you've no doubt heard countless times before. In practicing diversification, you seek to own a group of securities, which is independent from one another. In investments, you may diversify by owning real estate, stocks, bonds and money market funds. The theory is that as one asset class does well the others might not do as well and thus your risk of loss is lowered by the fact you hold all four. Or, you may and usually do diversify within each asset class. That is you may own bonds from different issuers (US Government, corporate or municipal) and which have different maturity dates. Maturity is the point in time in which you are usually paid back your original invested funds. When it comes to stocks, you may take ownership in a variety of ways in order to diversify. Owning several mutual funds is a good example and so is owning different stocks outright. Maybe you own General Electric, Dow Chemical, Exxon, IBM and Merck which all happen to be stocks part of the Dow Jones Industrial Average. As such you have practiced diversification, as you have ownership in different corporations and in widely different industries. At times, certain industries do better than others and prosper. In having an equity stake spread across different businesses you are practicing diversification or spreading your risk of exposure to any one industry. An example of not being diversified is putting most of your hard-earned capital into one single investment, whatever it may be, like the newly advertised emerging market "Tasmania Fund." The problem arises if Tasmania doesn't emerge and the fund loses 64% of its market value for the year. You weren't diversified because you had most of your "eggs" in one basket. You had no other investments to cushion your loss. You were unfortunately left exposed to your one investment's performance for the year. (If you got this advice from your broker he won't be your broker for long and not because you fire him either. That broker has violated several rules of conduct and should be promptly shown the door on a permanent basis by his boss.)

Yes, diversification is important to you as an investor. But, you really don't need to own many different investments in order to achieve it. As we have shown, it makes no difference if you own thirty or 500 stocks in your efforts to create wealth over an extended period of time. The fact that the two indexes perform in similar fashion over time implies diversification is reached in owning just thirty stocks. I'll venture to say that all you really need is to build a portfolio of five to eight stocks across several industries and you'll be properly diversified with returns to match or mirror the S & P 500, the Dow or any other index you chose to replicate. Michael Sivy and Brian P. Murphy in the November 1999 issue of *Money* magazine concur in writing, "And the number of stocks you must own to diversify properly is quite small—between eight and fifteen."[1]

One of the key principles to building wealth is to not entrust your hard-earned capital to the "middleman" for investment decisions. You, the investor will suffer over the long run. A significant portion of your return will go into the pockets of the middleman at your expense. Yes, I am speaking about the mutual fund and brokerage industry. The investment managers that go along with it. The analysts and the brokers.

Did you ever wonder how these prominent investment firms could afford such lavish and high priced office space? And I don't mean just in New York City where many of the firms are headquartered. Merrill Lynch, Morgan Stanley Dean Witter and Painewebber for example have offices throughout the United States and abroad. From my own experience, I worked in Beverly Hills, CA in fine office space for Morgan Stanley Dean Witter. Beverly Hills, I have found, has nothing cheap to offer. I'm sure the offices in Greenwich, CT, downtown San Francisco or Tokyo don't come without a high price tag either. Yes, the investment business has been very good and very profitable for a number of years. The middle person in high priced Armani and Chanel suits and Rolex watches want to keep it that way. And why not? They like their family trips to the Hamptons in New York. The investment conference in mid-February in Orlando, Florida is a welcome relief from the blizzard in the East. The week of skiing in Vail or Aspen Colorado is delightful for the kids each March. The six and sometimes seven figure year-end bonuses are welcomed and helpful additions. These profits are in large measure derived from investors like you and me across America.

I don't think it has to be that way. Especially when the investment firms and mutual fund companies provide so little to us. The American public is being fleeced!! I hope you, too, conclude that very few of their services are needed. Let's find out why. Let's find out how the investment public is being taken advantage of? Let's begin to change our investment practices and let us control our own destiny. Let's learn and listen to the great minds on Wall Street. Let's just refuse to give them our hard-earned capital and power to decide what to do with it. We deserve better!!

The mutual fund industry has grown significantly over the last decade. There are now reported to be more mutual funds in existence than there are issues of common stock on the exchanges. That means there now exists about 7,000 mutual funds. The growth and popularity in funds have come from several areas. First, the market has been very kind to investors over the last decade, as the market has appreciated considerably. This has spurred demand by the public to enter and invest in the market. New financial products have been made to fill the increased demand. Second, corporations have increasingly adopted and promoted 401(K) plans. These are employee retirement plans in which the employee directs the investable funds. The old-line company pension plan has been largely put to pasture. In many cases the employee has a choice of four or five different mutual funds in which to invest and that's it. Mutual fund companies love this business because stable long-term associations with the fund company usually results. The mutual fund company has a built in long-term profit center since retirement money is usually invested for many years. Lastly, there are so many mutual funds today because it is a highly profitable business.

Just look at the dollars spent on promotions to attract your funds. Wherever you look there are ads. Ads in newspapers, magazines, radio, TV and the Internet. I've even seen ads on billboards, park benches and at bus stops promoting investment companies. Pretty soon, you'll see a mutual fund company advertise on a Wheaties box. And guess who is paying for all this promotion? That's right you, the investor! The promotional dollars spent and the fees and profits the fund companies generate are taken out of the investor's hide. Let's see how.

If mutual funds performed well in relation to the Standard and Poors 500 index or the Dow Jones, then supporting the handsome salaries and bonuses the middleman gets wouldn't be so bad. But, the truth is very few mutual funds provide returns greater than the indexes. Chart 4 provides us a very good illustration of this fact.

CHART 4

General Equity Funds Outperformed by the Standard and Poor's 500 Index
1963 - June 30, 1998

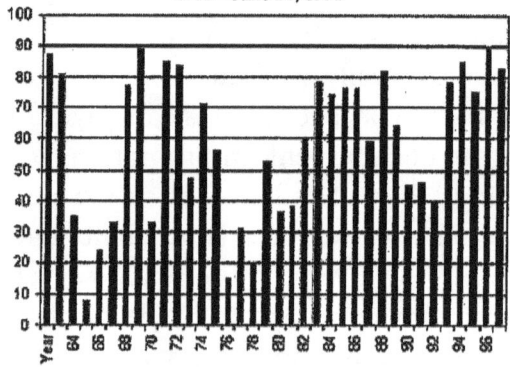

According to an article by columnist Bill Barker entitled, "The Performance of Mutual Funds," "approximately 80% of mutual funds underperform the stock market's returns in a typical year. Over the past couple of years, that number has been going up, as mutual funds have been raising their fees to even higher levels."[2] Chart 4 outlines this picture clearly.

So what explains this differential in performance between the Standard and Poors 500 and the generic growth fund that invests primarily in stocks? One would think those Harvard MBA's could do a better job for us, the investing public.

There are many important reasons why so many stock funds perform so poorly in relation to the indexes.

The typical equity fund holds somewhere between eighty and one hundred different stocks in its portfolio. Earlier, it was shown that the number of stocks one holds has about zero correlation to returns achieved. Owning thirty stocks produces the equivalent return of 500. Therefore, owning shares in a mutual fund, which owns eighty to one hundred different stocks, adds no value to enhancing returns. Diversification, in of itself, breeds average or index performance. And that's what most mutual funds are—average performers. Eight out of ten funds don't even match the S & P 500 returns. Most large company oriented growth funds are comprised to various degrees of the same stocks which are found in the Dow Jones and the Standard & Poors 500. How can a mutual fund, as such, greatly outperform the index when it owns many of the same stocks in the index? The answer is it can't. Let's look at a few examples of mutual fund performance to set the record straight.

I have selected three different mutual funds from three different fund companies to compare and analyze. These three have been selected because they each have been in existence for quite some time and have a history of performance. Each is a growth fund. Each is in the top ten of all mutual funds in terms of size and assets and finally because

American Funds, Fidelity and Janus are highly publicized and recognized fund families.

The Investment Company of America, is a mutual fund and part of the American Funds Group, and came into existence in 1934. As of July 31, 1999 the fund's top ten holdings were as follows:

Time Warner	BankAmerica
Fannie Mae	Sprint
Philip Morris	AT & T
Viacom Cl B	IBM
Pfizer	AT & T Liberty Media CL A

Source: www.morningstar.com (August 15, 1999).

Three of the top ten holdings are part of the Dow Jones Industrial Average—Philip Morris, AT & T and IBM while all, excluding AT & T Liberty, are presently included in the S & P 500.

Fidelity's Magellan Fund, begun in 1963, is the fund the legendary Peter Lynch ran for so many years. Its top holdings were as follows as of March 31, 1999:

General Electric	Cisco Systems
Microsoft	Merck
MCI Worldcom	Citigroup
AOL	Wal-Mart
Home Depot	Time Warner

Source: Magellan Annual Report 1999

Four of the top ten holdings are part of the Dow Jones Average—General Electric, Merck, Citigroup and Wal-Mart and all ten are currently part of the S&P 500.

The Janus Fund began in 1970, and as of June 30, 1999, the top ten holdings were:

Cisco Systems	Linear Tech
Time Warner	Texas Instruments
Comcast Special CL A	American International Group
Sun Microsystems	Tyco International
Charles Schwab	American Express

Source:www.morningstar.com (August 15, 1999).

In this case only one stock is part of the Dow Jones—American Express while all, with the exception of Linear Technology, are part of the S&P 500.

Let me remind you that each fund owns other stocks in lesser quantities that are also part of the indexes. I have shown only a small sample of their holdings. Doesn't it seem kind of foolish to hire a mutual fund to pick stocks in the index and not achieve returns of the index? It is!! There are many reasons why this phenomenon occurs.

One of the major reasons why funds underperform the market is that they are holding some of their (your) money on the sidelines in cash. Let's take a look at the three funds we have mentioned before:

According to online services at: www. morningstar.com on August 26, 1999 Investment Company of America was reported to be holding 14.1% of its assets in cash as of July 31, 1999 and the Janus Fund was holding 9% in cash as of June 30, 1999. Upon inspection of Magellan Fund's Annual Report dated March 31, 1999 (p.25), it shows 6.6% of its assets being held as cash equivalents. Do you think 6.6% of the Magellan Fund is a lot of cash? Try $5.998 billion according to the Magellan Annual Report!

Now some times in history, cash, and other short-term investments like certificates of deposit, Treasury Bills, money markets, and commercial paper outperform the equity markets. It certainly happened in 1973—1974 when cash could actually earn 17% and the market dropped nearly 47%. But, over the long run cash returns don't deserve a place at the dinner table. Mutual fund managers like to keep funds in cash so that when redemptions occur (meaning when you want a check sent to you out of your account) it can come out of cash reserves. The fund managers are fearful of large-scale redemptions and don't want to be forced to sell stocks in a down market to pay customers back. Thus, the fund managers as a cushion keep cash positions on hand. Yet, recently I turned on the TV and heard an interview with a fund manager and the interviewer asked, "what is your investment philosophy?" What came out of the fund manager's mouth was a cliché I've heard forty or fifty times before and in part his answer was, " we like to remain fully invested." Well that's a good idea in principal, but in practice mutual funds sing another tune.

According to Bill Barker in his article, "Turnover and Cash Reserves," he states: "the annual rate of return on cash over the last 120 years or so has been about 4%."[3] That's certainly a lot less than the 18.21% annualized return for the S & P 500 for the last ten years through December 1999. The three funds we have looked at were holding a low of 6.6% and a high of 14.1% assets in cash. This figures closely to what Mr. Barker further states, "actively managed mutual funds don't invest all the money, but instead maintain cash balances of approximately 8%."[4]

So, here's what really happens when you invest in a mutual fund. Let's say you open account at Fidelity Investments with $5,000 and invest in one of their many growth funds. Maybe you chose the Magellan Fund. I don't care if you dig ditches for a living or write poetry or run a division of Microsoft, only 92%, or so, of your invested dollars will be exposed to equity appreciation. Meaning, of that $5,000 you thought you were putting into the market only $4,600 is at work for you. The other $400 or so is being held by the fund in cash. Yet when you invested didn't you want full exposure? The remaining 8% invested in cash will earn about 4% annually. I'd rather be 100% invested with the potential to earn 18.21%, than having 92% of my money at work and trying to play catch up. The indexes have no cash balances. Mutual funds do. Cash provides a drag on returns to mutual fund performance.

Now are you beginning to see why eight out of ten funds fail to match index performance?

Later in the book I will be making some suggestions on what you can do so that the money you want invested in the market is in fact almost 100% invested. Why pay a mutual fund and the Harvard MBA fund manager to hold on to your invested funds in cash? You probably shouldn't. If you want to hold on to cash, walk down to your neighborhood bank and open up a free checking account with interest. At least with the new account you could also get a free toaster oven.

There are two basic types of mutual funds from which to chose from. You can pay a broker or a fund company a sales charge for the privilege of owning the fund. These are called load funds. Or you can purchase a fund without a sales charge penalty. These are called no-load funds. If you intend, or are intent, in owning a mutual fund (I hope not) then make sure you purchase the no-load variety. Bill Barker in an article entitled, "Loads" states:

> When a broker recommends a fund for one of her clients to buy, that fund will be in all probability a load fund, and the load, or sales charge, is pocketed by the broker and/or middlemen as payment for the "service of helping you pick a good fund."
>
> You should be aware that there is no real difference historically between the performance of load funds and no-load funds in terms of year-to-year performance. In fact, according to the latest survey by the mutual fund data analyzer Morningstar, even excluding the drag on returns if the load were included in the calculation, no-load funds actually have a superior record to load funds over the last 3-year and 5-year periods.
>
> Let us repeat. FUNDS THAT IMPOSE NO COST TO PURCHASE HAVE OUTPERFORMED THOSE THAT

BROKERS PAY THEMSELVES TO FIND FOR THEIR CLIENTS.[5]

Isn't this interesting? Pay someone else something and get nothing in return for the service paid.

So, if you are going to invest in a fund don't hire anyone—do it yourself!

What are some of the other reasons mutual funds perform so poorly in relation to the Dow Jones Average or S & P 500? Remember that approximately 80% don't match index returns in any given year.

According to Fidelity Investments in its annual report of the Magellan Fund dated March 31, 1999 (p.4) the average growth fund had an average annualized return of 16.32% over the last ten years through the date above. The Fidelity report further shows the S & P 500 returned 18.98% during the same time period. That's leaving quite a bit of money on the table the last ten years for the privilege of having the middleman on Wall Street invest your hard-earned dollars, as we shall see. The roughly 2.5% differential adds up to no small pocket change over time (assuming rates of return remain constant).

Growth of $10,000	Rate of Return	Last 10 Years	Next 10 Years	Next 20 Years
Average Growth Fund	16.32%	$45,300	$205,600	$932,400
S & P 500	18.98%	$56,800	$323,200	$1,837,000

As I mentioned earlier, nothing matters more to wealth creation than the compounded annualized return you achieve and the length of time you obtain it. The seemingly small 2.5% difference in your return can certainly alter your retirement plans. Again, I'd rather have the extra $904,600 in my pocket in thirty years for retirement, for my grandchildren (if any) and for any charitable grants I wish to make. Maybe you feel the same way?

In relation to the Standard & Poors 500 index, the average American who has invested in the "average performing growth fund" has and could continue to lose significant wealth while the fund companies prosper and get rich on our dollars. So, maybe it's time to start thinking twice about investing in a mutual fund should they come knocking?

How have our three chosen funds performed over a similar time frame? Charts 5, 6 and 7A shows the performance of Investment Company of America, The Janus Fund and the Magellan Fund. The Charts are depicted through year-end 1999.

CHART 5

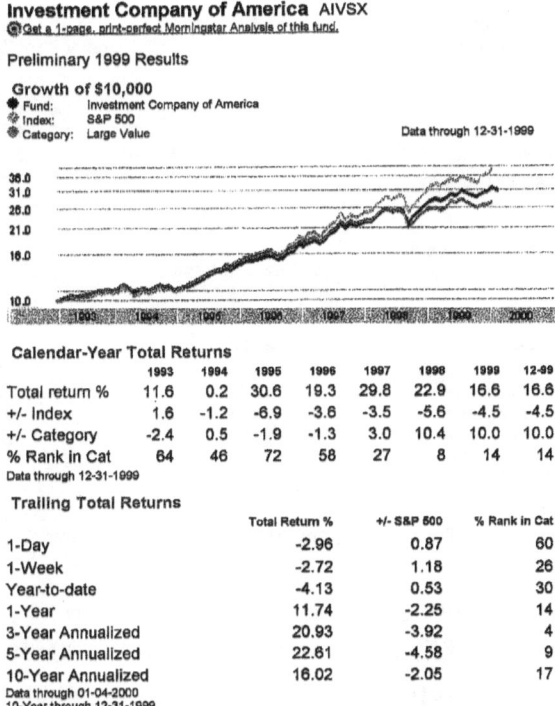

Investment Company of America AIVSX

ⓖ Get a 1-page, print-perfect Morningstar Analysis of this fund.

Preliminary 1999 Results

Growth of $10,000

◆ Fund: Investment Company of America
✦ Index: S&P 500
● Category: Large Value

Data through 12-31-1999

Calendar-Year Total Returns

	1993	1994	1995	1996	1997	1998	1999	12-99
Total return %	11.6	0.2	30.6	19.3	29.8	22.9	16.6	16.6
+/- Index	1.6	-1.2	-6.9	-3.6	-3.5	-5.6	-4.5	-4.5
+/- Category	-2.4	0.5	-1.9	-1.3	3.0	10.4	10.0	10.0
% Rank in Cat	64	46	72	58	27	8	14	14

Data through 12-31-1999

Trailing Total Returns

	Total Return %	+/- S&P 500	% Rank in Cat
1-Day	-2.96	0.87	60
1-Week	-2.72	1.18	26
Year-to-date	-4.13	0.53	30
1-Year	11.74	-2.25	14
3-Year Annualized	20.93	-3.92	4
5-Year Annualized	22.61	-4.58	9
10-Year Annualized	16.02	-2.05	17

Data through 01-04-2000
10-Year through 12-31-1999

CHART 6

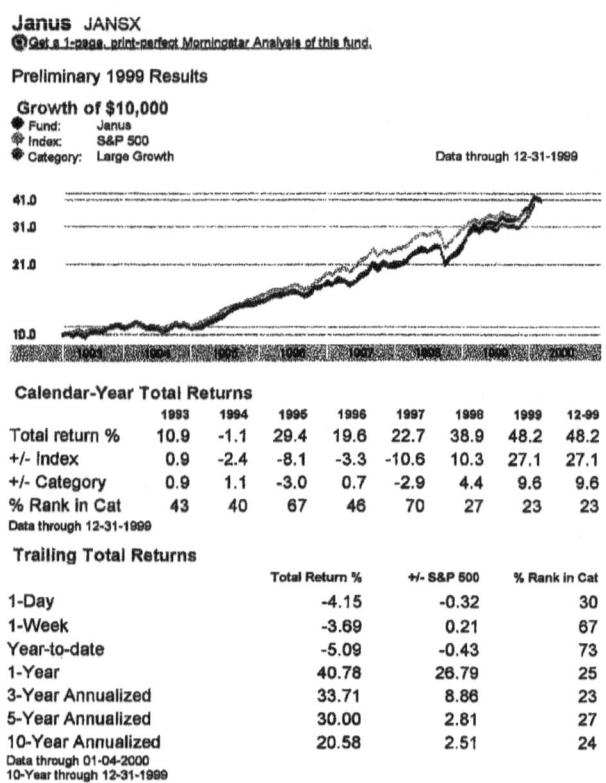

Janus JANSX
ⓡ Get a 1-page, print-perfect Morningstar Analysis of this fund.

Preliminary 1999 Results

Growth of $10,000
● Fund: Janus
❋ Index: S&P 500
◆ Category: Large Growth

Data through 12-31-1999

Calendar-Year Total Returns

	1993	1994	1995	1996	1997	1998	1999	12-99
Total return %	10.9	-1.1	29.4	19.6	22.7	38.9	48.2	48.2
+/- Index	0.9	-2.4	-8.1	-3.3	-10.6	10.3	27.1	27.1
+/- Category	0.9	1.1	-3.0	0.7	-2.9	4.4	9.6	9.6
% Rank in Cat	43	40	67	46	70	27	23	23

Data through 12-31-1999

Trailing Total Returns

	Total Return %	+/- S&P 500	% Rank in Cat
1-Day	-4.15	-0.32	30
1-Week	-3.69	0.21	67
Year-to-date	-5.09	-0.43	73
1-Year	40.78	26.79	25
3-Year Annualized	33.71	8.86	23
5-Year Annualized	30.00	2.81	27
10-Year Annualized	20.58	2.51	24

Data through 01-04-2000
10-Year through 12-31-1999

Source: Reprinted by permission of Morningstar, Inc.

The first graph depicts the growth of $10,000 in Investment Company of America in relation to the S & P 500. It clearly shows through the period represented on the graph that the fund has underperformed in relation to the index. Through December 1999 the ten year annualized return has been 16.02%—less than the average growth fund return of 16.32% reported above. Again through December 31, 1999, the S & P reported return was 18.21%.

Second is a graph depicting the growth of $10,000 in the Janus Fund. Janus returns have been better as we can judge for ourselves. In fact, over the last ten-year period through December 31, 1999, Janus sported an annualized return of 20.58%, about 2.5% higher than the S & P 500 over a similar time frame. Does this mean the Janus Fund has been and is a superior investment to the S & P 500? Looking at the returns you would think so. But there is more to the story that we will uncover shortly. Suffice it to say for now that the Janus Fund is one of those rare funds for the last ten years with top performance in surpassing the S & P 500. Soon we shall see why the Janus Fund reported returns are just a smoke screen to the investing public—that you, the investor, really aren't receiving the whole 20.58% return claimed by the fund company.

CHART 7A

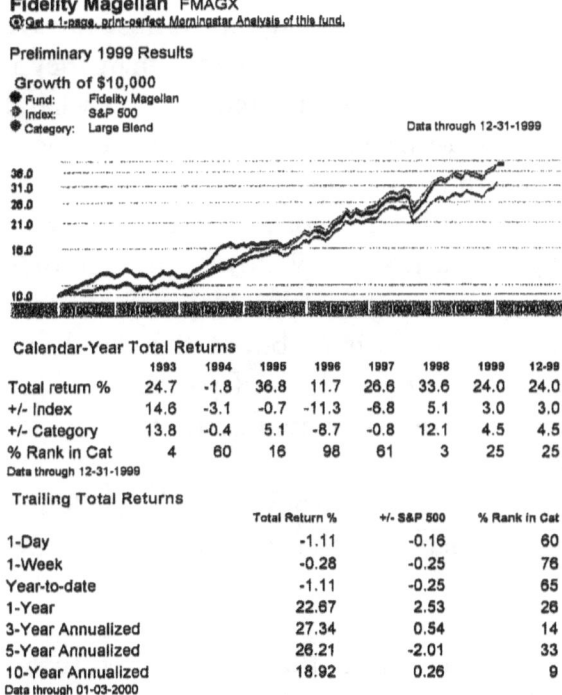

Fidelity Magellan FMAGX
ⓘ Get a 1-page, print-perfect Morningstar Analysis of this fund.

Preliminary 1999 Results

Growth of $10,000
● Fund: Fidelity Magellan
◆ Index: S&P 500
● Category: Large Blend

Data through 12-31-1999

Calendar-Year Total Returns

	1993	1994	1995	1996	1997	1998	1999	12-99
Total return %	24.7	-1.8	36.8	11.7	26.6	33.6	24.0	24.0
+/- Index	14.6	-3.1	-0.7	-11.3	-6.8	5.1	3.0	3.0
+/- Category	13.8	-0.4	5.1	-8.7	-0.8	12.1	4.5	4.5
% Rank in Cat	4	60	16	98	61	3	25	25

Data through 12-31-1999

Trailing Total Returns

	Total Return %	+/- S&P 500	% Rank in Cat
1-Day	-1.11	-0.16	60
1-Week	-0.28	-0.25	76
Year-to-date	-1.11	-0.25	65
1-Year	22.67	2.53	26
3-Year Annualized	27.34	0.54	14
5-Year Annualized	26.21	-2.01	33
10-Year Annualized	18.92	0.26	9

Data through 01-03-2000

Source: Reprinted by permission of Morningstar, Inc.

The Magellan Fund provided investors with a ten-year average return of 18.92% while during the same period the S & P returned 18.21% through December 1999. Again, the return is commendable for Magellan as it surpassed the S & P for the same period. Remember that usually no more than 20% of all funds surpasses index performance in any given year. But, as with the Janus Fund the return figure is distorted to confuse the investor. Shortly we shall see how.

One of the interesting points to mention is that of the three funds discussed only one is a no-load fund. Guess which fund that is? Well if you were thinking the one with the highest return you were correct. That's right the Janus Fund. This bears out the point discussed earlier that no-load funds tend to outperform commissioned funds.

The mutual fund industry has created some sophisticated terminology to explain simple concepts. This terminology although accurate in its definition can mislead and confuse the average investor. In essence things are made to sound better than they really are. You believe the fund company and fund manager know what they are doing. You entrust your hard-earned capital to the men or women in the expensive suits. You think they are intelligent so they must know what they are doing. I mean they use words you've never even heard. Maybe you get a feeling of trust, security, power, prestige or simple elation because you are a proud owner of the Magellan or Janus Fund. These are certainly nice feelings to have, but in the world of investing they provide little if any added wealth. So if you've ever heard or read the words "turnover" or "turnover rate" and had no idea what they meant—you are not alone.

Bill Barker in his article, "Turnover and Cash Reserves," provides some interesting comments which I couldn't say any better and deserves attention:

> To every fund, there is turnover, turnover, turnover. And knowing the historical turnover of your fund

choice is a necessary step to understanding the likely performance of a fund over time.

A fund's turnover rate basically represents the percentage of a fund's holdings that change every year. "Turnover" is the gross proceeds from all sales divided by the total assets in the mutual fund.[6]

Mr. Barker in the same article continues in saying, "In plainer English, turnover represents how much of a mutual fund's holdings are changed over the course of a year through buying and selling. Managed mutual funds have an average turnover rate of approximately 85%, meaning that funds are turning over nearly all of their holdings every year. Many funds, in fact, have turnover ratios of more than 100%, meaning their average holding period for a stock is less than one year."[7]

In even plainer English, you've entrusted your savings to mutual fund companies and their "pros" who exhibit neurotic behavior in their buying and selling practices. I recently saw an interview on television with a mutual fund manager in a dark suit and he was asked the question, "What is your turnover rate?" To which the well-educated "investment pro" responded, " Our fund has a turnover rate of about 80%." I was brought up with the notion when you invest in the stock market it is for a long period of time and maybe for the investor's lifetime. The typical growth fund exhibits any thing but this behavior. I don't equate selling 80% of your holdings in a year with the term "investment pro" or "mutual fund manager." What the fund manager is really doing is that he is selling eight out of ten stocks he currently holds in your portfolio during the course of the year. Then the fund manager invests in something else and does the same thing over and over again. What the fund companies really do is speculate and not invest your hard-earned capital. When you buy a mutual fund you are buying a group of stocks on a diversified and speculative basis. I believe short-term investment practices equate to speculation and not proper investment behavior.

So, you've hired a bunch of guys on Wall Street to rent stock and not own it on your behalf when you "invest" in a mutual fund. You may own shares in a mutual fund for a long period of time but the underlying stocks owned by the fund are usually here today and gone the next quarter. The following table is constructed from data through Morningstar and illustrates the point of turnover and turnover rates among the ten largest equity funds:

Fund	Total Assets (In Billions)	Turnover Rate
Fidelity Magellan	$97.5	34 %
Vanguard 500 Index	$92.6	6 %
Washington Mutual Investors	$58.6	18 %
Investment Company of America	$54.5	25 %
Fidelity Growth and Income Fund	$50.5	29 %
Fidelity Contrafund	$43.5	220 %
Vanguard Windsor II	$35.2	31 %
American Century Ultra Investors	$34.9	128 %
Janus Fund	$32.3	70 %
Vanguard Wellington Fund	$27.1	29 %

Source:www.morningstar.com (September 15, 1999).

The lowest turnover rate is the Vanguard 500 Index Fund because the fund simply holds the S & P 500 index and changes are only necessary when the index undergoes changes. The other large funds can be classified as actively managed equity funds. The average turnover rate of these other nine funds is about 65%. A little less than Mr. Barker's estimate of 85%, but nonetheless significant.

Ross Perot was clearly correct in his comments about Wall Street when he said, "they are paying a bunch of twenty-eight year-old kids with MBAs $400,000 a year and they don't know what they are doing." No where else are his words more accurate in describing the investment behavior and "turnover" exhibited by mutual funds and its highly priced fund manager. Supposedly, investment companies hire some of the best and brightest to serve you. They have layers of research analysts with the noble intentions of recommending and commenting on most of the leading publicly held corporations. The analysts are there to assist the fund manager in his or her asset selection. You'd think the research, time and effort would be put to good use by the fund manager. You would think that sound long-term investment decisions are being made by the fund manager based on a company's financial performance, a strong balance sheet, long-term growth prospects etc.. But, given all these great resources and minds the fund manager has to draw upon, the typical fund manager acts like a chicken with its head cut off.

You, again, are hiring a fund manager to rent stock for you—not own. The higher the turnover rate a fund has, the more stock you are renting during the course of a year. It seems ludicrous to me that a mutual fund can actually like and hold General Electric in its portfolio, say in January, and then later in the year sell some or all of it. Remember that the average mutual fund sells 80% of its portfolio during the course of a year according to Mr. Barker. Now, a stock like General Electric has been around since 1892. It is part of the Dow Jones Industrial Average. The company is currently the first or second most valuable corporation in the United States based upon the amount of stock outstanding at its current market price of $145 per share as of December 1999. That equates to a current market value over $400 billion. According to Standard & Poors through September 1999, General Electric has had an annualized return of 38.4% for the previous five years and about 26% for the last ten. Chart 7 depicts the returns of General Electric in relation to the S & P 500 index. You don't have to be a rocket scientist to figure out that General Electric has been a very worthwhile investment for a great number of years. It has obviously outperformed the index and by quite a large margin.

CHART 7

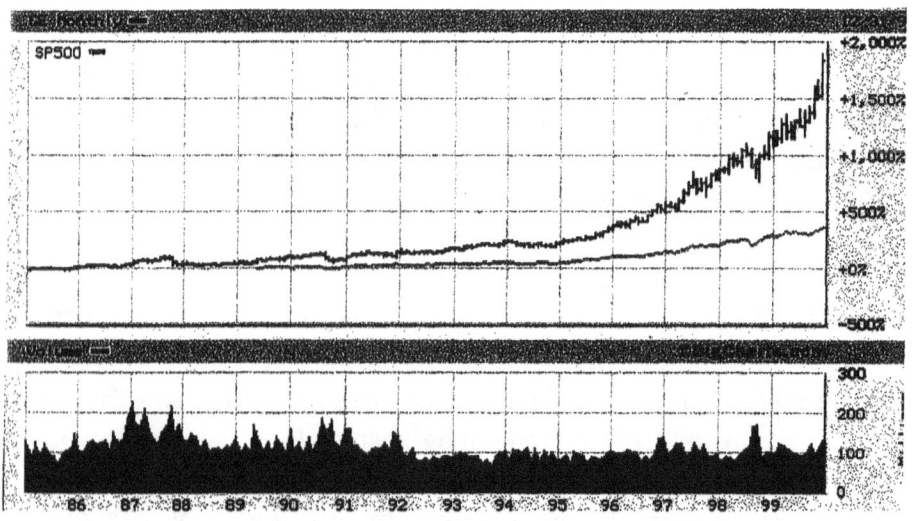

General Electric has been in business over one hundred years, manufacturing items from light bulbs and refrigerators to jet engines. I can't imagine companies like General Electric are good investments one month and become bad ones almost overnight. Yet, mutual funds in many cases treat these fine companies as such. Holding a stock for less than a year, like General Electric, makes no sense to me. I don't believe a company that has been in business over one hundred years can be such a great investment early in the year and by late fall sold or reduced to rubble in the mutual fund's portfolio. These shortsighted buy/sell actions by mutual fund managers are wrong. Once again these actions are known as "turnover" and turnover to me is inherently illogical. When a mutual fund exhibits the normal 85% turnover rate, the fund "operator" is outwardly expressing neurotic behavior. In physics, this can be compared to the term "hyper-kinetic energy" or wasted energy through effort. I believe turnover is an exercise in futility or "wheel spinning." When a fund exhibits such a high turnover rate I don't think we can be so kind and call the person in charge the "fund manager." A more appropriate term is "fund operator" because your funds are being anything but managed. They are in reality being rented. Renting stock is not the mechanism to achieve superior investment results. Long-term ownership can be, as we shall see. Not only are these the actions of a neurotic individual they're also severely detrimental to you, the investor, as we shall see too.

While I was at Morgan Stanley Dean Witter we used to have (and I imagine they still do) fund managers speak to us about the merits of this or that particular growth fund. Nine out of ten times I'd say to myself, "Here comes another fund operator to visit us in Beverly Hills in February. It must be cold in the East. Gee isn't it funny we never see these guys in summer." I got pretty proficient in sizing up the hype created within the firm over a particular fund. In a nutshell, if the firm was intent on selling and promoting a particular fund then it's probably a good idea I should avoid it. If the track record of performance was less than the S & P 500 and the turnover rate was the normal 85% or so, then I wanted no part of it for myself or my clients. At Morgan Stanley Dean Witter these attributes seemed to always be present. So, when the men and women wearing the Armani and Chanel suits and Rolex watches came through the door I sort of tuned out. I guess you can gather by now that I am not a big fan of mutual funds.

Now let's take a look at our three chosen mutual funds namely, Investment Company of America, the Janus Fund and the Magellan Fund and see what sort of turnover rates and "investment" decisions the fund managers have been making.

TURNOVER %

	1993	1994	1995	1996	1997	1998
Investment Co. Of Am.	18	31	21	17	26	25
Janus Fund	127	139	118	104	132	70
Magellan Fund	155	132	120	155	67	34

Source: Morningstar Mutual Funds (1999), 208, 229 and 415.

As we can judge for ourselves the Janus and Magellan Funds exhibit a similar level of turnover or trading activity. The average for the six-year period (1993-1998) has been 115% for Janus and 110% for Magellan. These turnover rates exceed the 85% average figure for growth funds according to Mr. Barker. The rates bear out the point that your funds are being rented by the middleman for periods less than a year as the turnover rates exceed 100%. If the historical returns of either fund greatly exceeded the S & P 500, by 2%-3%, then owning them might make some sense. However, this is simply not the case. I do not see the logic in handing over my investable capital to the fund "pro" to make short-term speculations on funds in which I am seeking long term appreciation. I hope you feel the same way I do.

Taking a look at Investment Company of America you'd hope to find that given a lower turnover rate averaging about 23% over the six year period (which is exceedingly low by mutual fund standards), a higher annualized rate of return to shareholders. However, we've shown earlier that the performance of Investment Company of America has lagged behind both the Janus and Magellan funds. One major reason can explain this inferior performance relative to the other funds. That is, the fund has been holding onto more of investor's money in cash and cash has provided a drain on returns.

So, here are some of the recent "investment decisions" the current fund managers have been making. The Janus Fund share changes are for a two-month period from February 1, 1999 through March 31, 1999.

JANUS FUND			
James P. Craig III since 1986			
* Bought	1999 % Change	* Sold	1999 % Change
Microsoft	69.4	Cisco Systems	128.6
Comcast Sp. CL A	77.3	Charles Schwab	35.6
Pfizer	(21.5)	Maxim	110.6
AIG	40.2	Costco	26.5
American Express	61.7	McKesson	(70.8)
AOL	97.9	EMC	157.1
General Electric	52.0	Time Warner	15.2
Enron	55.3	Linear Tech.	58.0
Tyco In'l	(1.8)	Bank of NY	.6
Sunmicrosystems	268.4		

* Source: www.morningstar.com (August 15, 1999).

The share changes for Investment Company of America is over a four-month period from December 1, 1998 through March 31, 1999.

INVESTMENT COMPANY OF AMERICA			
A Management Team			
* Bought		* Sold	
Philip Morris	(55.7)	Time Warner	15.2
Viacom	60.0	Fannie Mae	(16.4)
AT&T	(0.4)	IBM	18.0
Pfizer	(21.5)		
First Union	(45.0)	Wal-Mart	66.7
Royal Dutch	26.1	Washington Mut.	(31.9)
DuPont	22.7	Wells Fargo	1.7
Merck	(8.1)	Texas Instruments	131.8
Monsanto	(24.9)	Deutsche Telekom	116.8
Cendant	34.3	Chase Manhattan	10.5

* Source: www.morningstar.com (August 15, 1999).

The Magellan Fund share changes are represented for the year from March 31, 1998 through March 31, 1999.

MAGELLAN FUND			
Bob Stansky since 1996			
* Bought		* Sold	
General Electric	52.0	Cisco Systems	128.6
Microsoft	69.4	Wal-Mart Stores	66.7
MCI Worldcom	11.5	Boeing	26.4
AOL	97.9	Ford	(8.7)
Home Depot	63.8	DaimlerChrysler	(20.1)
Merck	(8.1)	Royal Dutch	26.1
Citigroup	67.0	Unocal Corp.	15.8
Time Warner	15.2	Mellon Bank	(0.5)
DuPont	22.7	Merrill Lynch	22.7
Chevron	3.1	Columbia/HCA	16.4
Philip Morris	(55.7)	Lucent	36.2

* Source: Magellan Fund Annual Reports 1998 & 1999

Source: Data for all 1999 returns from the *Los Angeles Times*, 2 January 2000, Business section.

Upon inspection of the preceding table several interesting points can be discerned. First, these are just a representative sample of the buying and selling occurring within each fund over a relatively short period of time. The stocks shown traded above are some of the larger positions changed within each fund. Second, the stocks, are in general household names, and are not fly-by-night concerns. Many of the stocks listed above are part of the Dow Jones Industrial Average and the S & P 500 (see Appendix A). Third, some of the stocks being sold by one fund company are actually being purchased by another. For example, Texas Instruments was being bought by the Janus Fund and at approximately the same time was being sold by Investment Company of America. Time Warner was being purchased by Magellan and at an equivalent point in time was being sold by the Janus Fund and Investment Company of America. Lastly, all this buying and selling activity conducted by the "fund operators" does not appear to amount to much. For all you statistical experts out there, there doesn't appear to be a high degree of correlation between the buy/sell decisions and short term return performance. Some of the stocks purchased have done quite well recently (such as AOL, Texas Instruments and Sun Microsystems) while others have fallen below the line and have shown negative returns (such as First Union, Merck, Monsanto, Pfizer and Philip Morris). The same can be said for stocks sold. Some stocks disposed of really took a beating and made the "fund operators" appear like fortunetellers (McKesson and Washington Mutual). However, some companies should never have been sold and have greatly outperformed the markets in 1999 (Deutsche Telekom, Cisco, Lucent, Maxim, Media One, Charles Schwab and Wal-Mart). Here the "fund operators" appear no smarter than monkeys. Looking at the sampling above there does not appear to be any pattern of success to the trading activity. Yet, one would think with the massive brain power on Wall Street and energy put forth in stock selection the results would be greatly superior to market returns over both a short and long term horizon. At least it seems logical to think this way. However, for a variety of reasons already put forth and eluded to, the fund manager's actions are inconsequential and without value to the mutual fund owner. To me, and I hope to you by now, it does not appear logical to buy a Microsoft one day and sell a Fannie Mae the next, followed by buying a General Electric and then selling a Wal-Mart Stores a week from last Tuesday. The point is that doing nothing with a portfolio of stocks owned seems to make a heck of a lot of sense.

According to the Los Angeles Times on January 2, 2000, the Dow Jones Industrial Average had posted a prior year return of 25.22% while the S & P 500 garnished 21.04%. With all the buying and selling these three actively managed funds did, they showed returns through the same date according, again, to the Los Angeles Times of: 16.56% for Investment Company of America, 48.19% for the Janus Fund and 24.05% for Magellan. Only the Janus Fund bested the Dow Jones Average for 1999. The other two funds fell short. As an investor you would have been better off simply owning the Dow and it isn't actively managed. There are no Harvard MBA's attempting to make logical and educated decisions concerning portfolio holdings with the thirty stocks represented in the Dow Jones Industrial Average. Shortly we shall see how the returns are in most circumstances lower to the investor than the fund company typically reports. This is meant to confuse you and me. You need to be able to read the fine print and understand mutual fund returns. The problem for the most part is you can't find the print to begin with.

Wall Street supposedly hires some of the best and brightest to manage funds and analyze stocks in the funds. They have jobs (you would think) to make educated and timely decisions in the investor's best interest. But, how do these timely "investment decisions" followed by the middleman help to add to the bottom line for the shareowners? They don't!

What is truthfully happening with your funds is diversified stock speculation. That is the timing of purchases and sales of many stocks being held on a relatively short-term basis. If the typical equity fund holds between eighty to one hundred different stocks how can the manager understand and properly evaluate, even through assistance, the intricacies of each company? I believe it is an impossible task. I don't believe the fund "operators" can time with any degree of accuracy when to buy or sell a specific stock. And yet this is magnified to about eighty times where eight out of ten stocks are changed during the year in the portfolio. Nonetheless, the general investing public is led to believe these are investment "pros" so therefore they must know what they are doing. Money magazine in its October 1999 issue relates an interview it had with Don Phillips, Chief Executive Officer of Morningstar Inc. The question was, "How important is portfolio turnover (to fund performance)?" Responded Mr. Phillips, "That's another key factor (to fund performance). We did an interesting study that showed pretty conclusively that higher turnover was almost always detrimental."[8] Clearly I'm not alone in my thinking when I say, we've been duped into thinking the middleman's efforts produce significant benefits to us.

You can gather I'm not the only person of sound mind and body to believe in and preach some of the investment principles within this book. Some very astute and successful investment pros do share many of my same opinions and beliefs I have about investing. For example, Mr. Phillips' short remarks. I'm not breaking any new ground here about investing. But, what I am doing am taking the time and energy to write about those beliefs and help spread the gospel throughout the land.

Recently, a very close friend of mine and business associate was quite upset at the office. I heard him ranting and raving about something. I asked him what it was all about. He said he was just getting into a heated discussion with his Morgan Stanley Dean Witter broker. He said, "Ted, how would you feel if you'd lost $400,000 trading stock on a portfolio worth about $1 million at the beginning of the year? And the market's gone up about twenty-some percent." To which I responded, " Well I don't think I'd shoot myself." Steve followed a pattern of speculative buying and selling over the course of several months. Call it bad luck, poor stock selection and timing and bad advice. But the point is Steve was buying and selling mostly well known and highly regarded stocks such as America On Line, Amazon.com, E*Trade and Dell Computer. Many of these same stocks are held in the various equity growth funds we have been discussing. Steve got caught up in the trading frenzy with Internet-related stocks, which has become so prevalent. The only difference between my friend Steve and the "fund operator" is that Steve speculated only with a few companies at once. Steve speculated in a concentrated non-diversified manner. Meaning he had most of his "eggs" in one or two baskets. If those few stocks or "eggs" performed well he could have been on a slow boat to China, but of course the opposite happened. A mutual fund on the other hand does not have the potential to cause the same degree of heartburn, which Steve experienced because the risk of significant loss (or superior gain) has been diversified away through the ownership of many more stocks. That may be the good news for the mutual fund. The bad news is the middleman operates in much the same manner as Steve— neurotic and compulsive by speculating in stock price movement over a short period of time.

The usual benefits advertised by the fund companies about the merits of investing in mutual funds are diversification, professional research and management and convenience. It's true that in a typical growth fund the investor does become diversified. Renting eighty or so stocks at once certainly accomplishes that task. But we've learned earlier that diversification can occur in ownership of many fewer stocks. The Dow Jones Average and the S & P 500 have performed almost identically for many years. The difference in the indexes is there are 470 fewer stocks comprising the Dow Jones Average. Again, return has nothing to do with the number of securities held. Later in the book I will outline better methods for you, the investor, to achieve more than ample diversification. Another merit the men on Wall Street lay claim to is "professional research and management." But why hire a mutual fund company and its "professional management" team to speculate and rent stock for you and in eight out of ten cases underperforms the market? I don't think you should. I know the claim is that investing in mutual funds is easy and convenient. "You may not have the time and inclination, "Mr. Investor," to invest yourself so we'll do it for you— don't worry we'll handle things for you. Just remember to send a check made payable to us and don't forget to include your social security number." Mutual fund investing is easy and convenient but you also pay for that right and "privilege"of share ownership. Don't forget a few percentage points of return in your favor over a long period of time can make all the difference in the world to you and your family.

Later, I will show you a few ways to invest which are just as easy and more importantly much more cost effective.

The neurotic trading practices of fund managers does not improve investment returns. It's a wasted effort in futility. In reality your returns are being diminished through trading and turnover but the fund companies find a way of not advertising these usual facts. Any time a mutual fund buys and sells a stock in its portfolio there is an implied capital gain (or loss). For example, you might decide to buy one hundred shares of AT & T stock at say $30 a share and later sell for a profit at $90 a share. Your gain was $60 per share wasn't it? No, not really. First, because commissions reduce your net gain. Second, and of much greater consequence to you is you are forced to pay to the government the capital gains tax on your $60 per share gain. The current tax law is written that if you hold an asset for less than a year the tax rate on your gain is the same rate you pay Uncle Sam on ordinary income such as wages, salaries and tips. For an individual earning $75,000 annually, the federal tax rate is a shade over 24%. This means of the $60 gain, Uncle Sam wants to be your partner and kindly requests its cut amounting to $1,440 or $14.40 per share. Therefore, you netted only a gain of $45.60 per share on an after-tax basis (And this example excludes any State tax you may obligated to pay in addition). Now that's a big difference from the $60 you would have received if

Uncle Sam hadn't gotten in your way. But as the old saying goes, "there are only two certainties in life—death and taxes." The good news from a taxing standpoint is that if the AT & T stock were held longer than one year the tax rate is reduced to 20% and Uncle Sam gets a smaller slice of the pie. So, your true or after-tax return is less than $60 per share no matter how you slice it. It means you have a lower rate of return on the invested funds than would be the case if there were no tax. It pays to be a long-term investor and not a short-term trader or speculator when taxes are an issue.

Unless you've invested in a tax deferred or retirement plan, mutual funds pass these same tax obligations on to you, the investor. Investors are mailed 1099 Forms annually. The form shows your amount of dividends received and the amounts of both short-term and long-term capital gains distributions generated through turnover. Again, you must pay tax to Uncle Sam or a new set of problems could arise. The men in the dark gray suits may come knocking. The tax you pay lowers your rate of return on your mutual fund investment. Just as it is lowered in the AT & T stock example. Turnover, does create capital gains tax exposure. You have to thank the mutual fund "operators" for lowering your return and wealth creation through turnover. Thank them, but be sure to blame yourself for entrusting your hard-earned capital to them in the first place.

Let's take a closer look at the problem of paying capital gains tax and how severely the tax may effect your returns and wealth creation.

Scenario 1:

You invest $1,000 on December 31, 1999 in a mutual fund of your choice. The fund for illustration purposes only owns one stock, Microsoft. The fund acquires 11.11 shares at $90 per share. The fund holds Microsoft all year. The stock rises over the next twelve months from $90 to $120. Your annualized percentage gain on Microsoft held by the fund is 33.3% and you still own the stock. Excluding a very small dividend payment by Microsoft your tax obligation to Uncle Sam is nil.

Your $1,000 invested in Microsoft is now worth $1,333. In year two, you start with $1,333 with the stock trading at $120 and by the end of the year 2001 the stock is trading at $150. The fund has held on to Microsoft for two full years. You've paid nothing out of your pocket for all practical purposes to the government during that time. You've gotten a two year annualized return on the Microsoft stock of 29% and your fund is now worth $1,666.

Scenario 2:

You invest $1,000 on December 31, 1999 in a mutual fund of your choice. Again the fund only owns one stock and this time it's Intel. The fund acquires 11.11 shares at $90 per share. The fund manager decides to sell the stock in July 2000. Thirty one days later he buys it back in August and then sells it again in late December. The stock rises from $90 in January to $110 in July and in August is repurchased at $100. At year-end the stock is selling at the same price as Microsoft at $120. What happens to you in this case? It's a bit more complex than Scenario 1. Because the fund manager sold Intel twice during the year you are most likely exposed to a higher capital gains tax rate than if Intel had been held longer than one year. Let's say your income is $75,000. This equates to a tax rate of 24%. First, you owe the tax on the gain from $90 to $110 when the stock was sold in July. On the $20 per share profit you owe Uncle Sam 24% of it or $4.80. When you buy the stock back in August at $100 you then owe the government its share when you sell Intel in December at $120. On the new $20 per share profit (from $100 to $120) you owe Uncle Sam another $4.80. So, when you get your 1099 at year end 2000 from the fund company it will show only minor income attributable to dividends (because Intel pays very little) but there will be a whopping short-term capital gains distribution of $40 per share (or $444.44.). You owe Uncle Sam $9.60 per share for the fund manager's trading efforts (or $106.66). Your $1,000 originally invested in Intel is now worth only about $1,225 because you had to pay capital gains tax of $9.60 per share. So, your after-tax gain is from $90 to $110.40 or ($120 less $9.60). Therefore, even though Microsoft and Intel performed exactly the same during the year your annualized rate of return was drastically reduced when viewed on an after-tax basis to 22.6%.

In year two, you are starting with $1,225 in cash because the fund manager has sold his position in Intel. Now the fund manager gets smart and decides to re-buy and hold Intel in the portfolio until hell freezes over, or he shakes hands with the little green men or until the Cubs win the World Series. The stock is bought back at $120 and twelve months later it is trading at $150 just like Microsoft. In year two there are no taxing consequences because Intel isn't sold. But, you've only invested $1,225 and could only acquire 10.2 shares of Intel trading at $120. At year-end your fund is worth $1,531, while in Scenario 1 the Microsoft stock is worth $1,666. In Scenario 2, you're poorer $135 over a two year period because of the capital gains tax you were forced to pay due to the trading practices of the fund manager. You've gotten a two year after-tax return of 23.7%. Not bad, but certainly not as attractive as the two year annualized return in Scenario 1 of 29%.

I hope the foregoing discussion proves to you that taxes have huge implications in the investment world.

Therefore, a much more accurate picture of return is your after-tax return. Meaning what you are left with following tax payments on dividends and capital gains. Believe me, mutual fund companies are well schooled and understand completely the notion of after-tax returns. It's just they don't like to mention it, print it or advertise about it. The same can be said about investment publications and magazines.

The total return and average annualized return figures the investment public is blitzed with by the fund companies on television, in magazines and over the Internet are pretax returns. Rarely are investors able to find returns on an after-tax basis as has been depicted in Scenario 2. You are constantly being painted a better picture than is actually the case. You are led to believe you are buying a "Van Gogh" but in actuality you are taking possession of a lesser-known artist's work.

You are being duped and misled by the investment community. Mutual fund companies rarely advertise after-tax (or lower) returns because they aren't required by law to do so. Why print lower returns if you don't have to—it doesn't sell as well. Since the fund companies are in fierce competition for your investment dollar, why talk about and publish information about an investor's real or honest rate of return? Maybe it's time for a change for the simple reason that it's the right thing to do.

Whenever, I pick up a magazine on investing such as *Money, Fortune, Forbes, Mutual Funds or Worth*, I almost always find commentary on the merits of this or that growth fund. I also find tables, charts and graphs showing the performance of the various funds as compared to the indexes over different time horizons. I find beautiful advertisements, in color, depicting returns for any number of different funds. But almost nowhere do I find these returns depicted on an after-tax basis.

Magazines, such as those listed above, are very hesitant to write the "whole truth" about mutual fund investment returns. They can not afford to piss-off the mutual fund companies. They need advertising dollars to exist and prosper. Mutual fund companies spend a tremendous amount on advertising to gain investor appeal and your money. The fund companies are clients of the magazine organizations. The two are linked at the hip. Both need each other. The last thing magazines care to do is to write scathing commentary on the mutual fund industry. To publish negative journalism about mutual funds' performance, fees, turnover and costs would be analogous to chopping-off the arm that feeds you. The almighty dollar is too important. I recently picked up a copy of the September 1999 issue of *Mutual Funds* magazine. Not only do you not find any negative articles about mutual fund investing; the magazine has the gall to print on its cover each month, "YOUR GUIDE TO AMERICA'S BEST INVESTMENTS." I'd certainly say that's a clever way to attract the ad dollars. In fact, I counted thirty different ads from fund companies in the issue and the magazine has only ninety-two pages. With that amount of revenue generated from fund advertising it's no wonder the magazine implies mutual funds are your best investment—**printed each and every month on the magazine cover.**

While I was at Morgan Stanley Dean Witter, I never once came across a broker talking to a client about the problems turnover creates with mutual fund investing. Nor, capital gains tax. Nor, the effect the tax has on lowering the investor's true rate of return. Simply put, the idea or notion of after-tax returns was shoved aside and under the rug. Either because these concepts required too much effort on the brokers part to convey to the clients, or for fear they may lose the sale, or for the simple reason the brokers didn't understand the concepts in the first place. For whatever reason, I never heard a broker paint a lesser picture to the client. Nor did I ever come across any literature printed by the firm about mutual fund investing viewed on an after-tax basis. All the fund prospectuses and glossy literature meant to inform and entice the investor never showed it. All the fund "operators" and analysts who visited us in Beverly Hills, meant to educate and inform the brokers, but not one mentioned or brought up this important detail.

How can those employed by the various fund companies speak honestly and fully inform the public about mutual fund investing? They can't! It's their livelihood. They are employed and paid handsomely to attract your dollar. I certainly wouldn't want to have a "Ted Lux" on my fund's payroll. So, the fund companies are quiet. The magazines and newspapers are all but silent. This author is on nobody's payroll. I can afford to tell the whole truth and nothing but the truth. I can say things those on the inside won't or can't discuss.

I agree entirely with Randy Befumo in his article entitled, "A Lesson in Tax Efficiency," found at motleyfool.com in late 1999 in which he states:

> The poor performance of the average mutual fund relative to the S & P 500 on a pre-tax basis has been

highly publicized over the past few years. A story that has been told a lot less is that on an after-tax basis, the returns get even worse. Index funds outperform money managers not only through minimizing expenses, but by staying invested and not changing those investments very often. Simply looking at the capital gains distributions in an index fund relative to other professionally managed money provides an object lesson about how low turnover and low cash balances can provide solid returns.[9]

Earlier we stated that about 80% of all equity funds underperform the S & P 500 annually. But, I forgot to mention those returns are reported on a pretax basis—not an after-tax basis! The same can be said for the returns shown for the Investment Company of America, the Janus and Magellan Funds and all other return numbers presented thus far. Believe it or not, according to the October 1999 issue of *Money* magazine (p.79), only one fund manager has been able to outperform the S & P 500 for eight consecutive years. His name is William Miller III and he runs the Legg Mason Value Trust fund.

So, if 80% of all equity funds don't match the return of the S & P on a pretax basis, can you imagine what percent exceeds the index on an after-tax basis? Certainly much smaller than 20%. Probably closer to 5% than 20% and here's why....

Earlier it was shown the average growth fund's annualized return to be 16.32% for the ten-year period ending March 1999, according to Fidelity Investments. The 16.32% is however on a pretax basis! Not after-tax! During a comparable period the S & P 500 returned 18.21%. Now there are no tax consequences with the index because it's the index. But with mutual fund ownership there certainly are. So, an investor really is not achieving 16.32% but something much less because of taxing issues. All the trading activity and stock spinning by the "fund operators" has been found to reduce an investor's annualized rate of return about 14%. Thus, on an after-tax basis the average mutual fund doesn't return 16.32% as earlier indicated, but rather 16.32 less 14% (and 14% of 16.32 equals 2.28%) equating to 14%. Fourteen percent is sure a lot lower than the 18.21% performance of the Standard & Poors 500.

The one place where an investor can find after-tax returns on mutual funds is through Morningstar reporting agency. These represent the true figures the investment public should be analyzing, screening and comparing. Not the ones published by the fund companies. Not the returns advertised in bold lettering in magazines and newspapers. The fact that Morningstar reports after-tax returns is a tribute to their organization. Specifically, in Morningstar's "Resource Guide" for 1999 it states:

Tax-Adjusted Return

The Tax-Adj Ret % column shows a fund's annualized after-tax total return for the three-, five-, and 10- year periods, excluding any capital-gains effects that would result from selling the fund at the end of the period. To determine this figure, all income and short-term (less than one year) capital-gain distributions are taxed at the maximum federal rate of 39.6% at the time of distribution. Long -term (more than one year) capital gains are taxed at a 20% rate. The after-tax portion is then reinvested in the fund. State and local taxes are ignored....

The "Resource Guide"continues by saying:

Pretax Return

The % Pretax Ret column provides a contrast to tax-adjusted historical return. While the latter measures the bottom-line after-tax results of a fund, without regard to pretax performance, the percentage pretax return statistic measures tax efficiency. This statistic (which excludes additional gains, taxes, or tax losses incurred upon selling the fund) is derived by dividing after-tax returns by pretax returns. The highest possible score would be 100%, which would apply to a fund that had no taxable distributions (such as many municipal-bond funds)...[10]

Let's take a look at how our three chosen funds have performed if we inspect after-tax performance. The following table is reconstructed from data published by Morningstar for fund performance for the ten-year period ending April 30, 1999.

	Total Return %	Tax Adjusted %	% of Pretax Return
Investment Co. Of Am.	16.83%	14.44%	85.8%
Janus Fund	19.71%	16.93%	85.9%
Magellan Fund	19.35%	16.18%	83.6%
Avg. of the Three	18.63%	15.85%	85.1%

Even though the fund companies report column 1 to you, you're really receiving returns closer to column 2. The average difference between Total (or Pretax) and Tax Adjusted Return is 2.78% among the three funds (that's close to 2.28% indicated above). On a tax-adjusted basis, none of the funds matched the performance of the S & P 500 (of 18.21%) for the ten-year period represented. This 2.78% differential may not seem like a big number to you but over time it can alter the course of your life. It detracts from your ability to create wealth to such a large degree that it's very hard to comprehend.

Let's see what happens to the growth of $10,000 for the next ten, twenty and thirty years should an investor be able to achieve the historical average of 18.63% in the future.

Growth of $10,000	Rate of Return	Pre Tax Future Value
10 Years	18.63%	$ 55,200
20 Years	18.63%	$ 304,700
30 Years	18.63%	$1,682,000

What happens to wealth creation on an after-tax basis assuming the 2.78% return adjustment remains constant and therefore the investor achieves the 15.85% average in future years.

Growth of $10,000	Rate of Return	After Tax Future Value
10 Years	15.85%	$ 43,500
20 Years	15.85%	$ 189,600
30 Years	15.85%	$ 825,800

It is quite apparent there is a huge discrepancy over time when the 2.78% adjustment is factored into the equation. At the end of thirty years the investor has earned $1,682,000, donated $856,200 to the government and has kept the remaining $825,800. The US Treasury Department has consumed more than 50% of the investor's return and didn't contribute a nickel to have such right. The fund investor has achieved less than half of his earnings potential, all thanks to the overzealous trading practices of the fund "managers."

By comparison, if the S & P 500 performs in the future as it has it in the past ten years through December 1999, returning 18.21%, an investor will create a much greater fortune by simply paralleling the index.

Growth of $10,000	Rate of Return	Future Value
10 Years	18.21%	$ 53,275
20 Years	18.21%	$ 283,800
30 Years	18.21%	$1,512,000

These numbers above would be wholly accurate for an investor if there were no tax consequences in owning the index. The S & P 500 however, as we have noted previously, undergoes changes each year as certain stocks are added and others are deleted by those in charge. These annual changes of approximately thirty stocks create potential capital gains tax for those trying to mirror the returns of the index. Thus, even though the index returns 18.21%, an investor would receive slightly less on an after-tax basis if S & P 500 ownership were possible. But how much less is the important question?

In a typical growth fund 85% of the portfolio is changed during the year. This 85% change causes about a 14% reduction from pretax return percentage to figure after-tax return percentage (if the investment is held outside a tax deferred plan). If the index has an average of thirty changes during the year it represents a very low turnover rate of 6% on 500 stocks (it's no coincidence the Vanguard 500 index fund has the same turnover rate). Six percent is certainly a lot less than 85%. Based on the ratio that 14 out of 85 is about 16.5%; then 16.5% of six is just about one. Therefore, it is reasonable to assume an investor would get only a 1% reduction from pretax return of 18.21% (or .182%) to find the after-tax return in S & P 500 ownership or approximately 18%. So, even viewed on an after-tax basis simply investing in and mirroring the S & P 500 seems to be the much better investment since the turnover rate is so low. I'd rather have an 18% after-tax return than 15.85% wouldn't you?

The first key to wealth creation through investment is to achieve the highest annualized rate of return possible for the greatest number of years. The second and newly added key to the chain is that it is best to achieve the return on an after tax basis. If you are intent on owning mutual funds (and I hope you are thinking twice about it) then please do it in a tax deferred retirement plan like an IRA or 401(k) plan. In either case there are no immediate taxing ramifications and issues. The third and final key element to wealth creation will be discussed a little later in the book.

Why is it the mutual fund managers, which I term "operators," act in such a neurotic fashion—turning over stock like a steak on a hot charcoal grill? Certainly the Harvard MBA's know better wouldn't you think? They do!

I doubt the average fund operator is truly neurotic. So, why the trading and inappropriate conduct which causes all investors to suffer? One reason is the trader has to justify his or her existence. To sit back and do nothing with the invested funds implies the investor is paying the mutual fund company handsomely for no action and advice. The investment companies hire large staffs to do research on many public companies. This is an ongoing exercise. Opinions and earnings estimates are made, changed and updated continually. To not follow the opinions and recommendations of your own in-house research staff would appear unusual to say the least. But, maybe by doing nothing or as little as possible is the best approach. In other words if the mutual fund "operator" is advised and guided to buy or sell XYZ Company, maybe he or she should walk away and do nothing.

The other reason for the neurotic behavior, and in defense of many mutual fund managers, is they are forced by law to sell or reduce exposure to any one particular company. Years ago, with noble intentions, lawmakers sought to protect the investing public by controlling and regulating the mutual fund industry. The major federal law designed to accomplish the task was The Investment Company Act of 1940. The Act provided for the newly created Securities and Exchange Commission to have various powers over mutual fund companies. One of the most important regulations, fully diversified investment companies must adhere to, is provided under Section 12 (d) of the 1940 Act which states in part:

> It shall be unlawful for any registered investment company (the "acquiring company") and any company or companies controlled by such acquiring company to purchase or otherwise acquire any security issued by any other investment company (the "acquired company"), and for any investment company (the "acquiring company") and any companies controlled by such acquiring company to purchase or otherwise acquire any security issued by any registered investment company (the "acquired company"), if the acquiring company and any company or companies controlled by it immediately after such purchase or acquisition own in aggregate—
>
> > ii. Securities issued by the acquired company having an aggregate value in excess of 5 per centum of the value of the total assets of the acquiring company;[11]

In plainer English, a mutual fund cannot have more than 5% of its assets tied up in one particular company. This provision has had the effect of creating and making sure most mutual funds are diversified and more than need be, according to this author.

At the time the law was created, a highly regarded investment theory was the "efficient market hypothesis" in which it was believed that no matter how much time, effort and energy anyone put forth to analyze and buy a stock it was meaningless. The opinion was that all information known or unknown about a company was already factored into the current price of a stock. Meaning what anyone paid for a company was the true value of the company. No bargains existed. Never was a company overpriced. Now, I do not believe this to be true. But with this pervasive thinking in 1940, lawmakers thought it best to protect the investing public through ample diversification and did so by creating the 5% rule. Under The Investment Act of 1940, it's apparent a diversified equity fund must hold at least twenty stocks in its portfolio to be law-biding. However, it's impractical for a mutual fund to own only twenty stocks. An immediate problem arises if a stock goes up in value. The fund "operator" is then required by law to pare back the interest the fund has in the particular stock to 5% of its holdings. Because of this law, mutual funds tend to own many more than twenty stocks with eighty to one hundred being the norm. The idea behind the law was, in part, to protect the investor through ample diversification. However, earlier it was shown there really is no difference in returns based on the amount of securities owned. Thirty stocks do the same trick as 500.

Let's look at an example of a mutual fund created ten years ago, owning one hundred different stocks. Assume each stock purchased was owned proportionately (therefore each stock represented 1% of the value of the fund). The mutual fund "operator" had constructed a very diversified equity fund. He or she had little or no problems in managing the fund and abiding to law as long a stock (s) didn't do too well.

Let's assume the growth fund manager was smart enough to buy Microsoft, Intel, Wal-mart Stores, The Gap, Berkshire Hathaway and Coke ten years ago. All of these companies have performed exceedingly well for shareowners over the last ten years. For example, if you had purchased one hundred shares of Microsoft stock in September 1989 at $68 per share costing about $6,800, ten years later, as of September 1999, you would own 7,200 shares priced at about $95 per share. Your worth in the stock would have grown from $6,800 to an amazing figure of $684,000. The stock went up in value about 10,000% in ten years or one hundred fold. Excluding the receipt of Microsoft dividends (which are negligible), the compounded annualized return equates to an astounding 58.58%. By comparison, if you had purchased one hundred shares of Intel in September 1989 priced at $32 per share and costing about $3,200, you would own 1,600 shares today ten years later. Priced at about $85 per share, your worth would have risen to the not too paltry sum of $136,000. Intel stock has risen about forty-two times in the last ten years. The annualized rate of return, although not as high as Microsoft, isn't too shabby at 45.5% (with the exclusion of dividends).

Believe it or not, the mutual fund "operator" would not have been able to hold most of these great performers in the portfolio for ten years even if he begged and screamed. Whereas, you the private investor could have! At some point their values would have risen above the 5% threshold. So, even though some of these stocks went up more than forty fold during the last ten years (like Microsoft and Intel), the mutual fund "operator" would have been forced to sell and pare back his positions. Meaning just when Bill Gates was in the midst of becoming the wealthiest man in the world through his appreciating Microsoft stock, this fund manager would not have been able to ride Mr. Gates' coattails even if he wanted to. The best the manager could have done would have been to ride the 1% interest in Microsoft or Intel or any of the other's mentioned to a 5% interest. Now a 500% increase is certainly an attractive number but it does fall far short of the 10,000% increase Microsoft experienced.

So, in diversified mutual funds this is an ongoing issue that confronts the fund managers. If an investment starts to do too well then he or she is required by law to reduce the position to 5% or less. This causes the fund "operators" to act (and I believe wrongly) and sell some of their best performing stocks. The sale of course creates potential capital gains tax, which is further detrimental to the investor. Because a fund manager is eventually forced to sell his winners, you can further digest why it's so difficult to match or top index performance. Be wary of blaming the fund "operator" for selling Microsoft, Intel, Dell Computers or Cisco Systems for he or she may be simply following the law. The point isn't why stocks like these are sold. The point is they are. **It is what it is.** Stocks like these are sold and it's usually to the investor's detriment.

In order to reduce turnover and to give investors a fair chance to beat the index, I believe a portion of The Investment Company Act of 1940 should be rewritten. Instead of a 5% maximum exposure of assets to any one particular company, I suggest the figure should be raised to 20%. Diversification, I believe would still be maintained, even with the potential for smaller portfolios. It would result in lower turnover and higher after-tax returns to investors. Most importantly, it's likely to diminish the neurotic behavior fund managers' exhibit because they would legally be able to hold on to their winners for a much longer period of time. I firmly believe amending this provision would significantly improve the performance of most mutual funds, thereby creating more wealth for the investor. Write your representative today!

So far we have seen the vast majority of equity funds underperform the market. The reasons why can be summed up below:

1. Diversification breeds mediocrity and reduces the potential for superior performance.
2. Sales charges or "loads" don't help out.
3. Cash balances are a significant drag on returns.
4. Fund "operators" "rent" stock. They tend not to invest. The high turnover rate associated is detrimental, pointless and unnecessary to investors.
5. Wealth can be created through long term equity ownership—not "rentalship."
6. Turnover can create potential capital gains tax which dramatically lowers returns.
7. The Investment Company Act of 1940 contains poor investment constraints.

The last item that provides for inferior performance is item number (8) and these are the costs associated with mutual fund ownership. As we shall see shortly, costs matter to fund performance. Please keep in mind just because a fund charges more does not assure superior performance. But one thing is for sure; a high cost fund will have to perform better to provide you the same return as a low cost fund. Like anything else in life you don't always get what you pay for. Maybe you should think twice about hiring the high priced lawyer in Beverly Hills or in Greenwich, CT to handle your divorce? Maybe you'd be better off hiring your retired uncle now living in Leadville, Colorado?

All businesses I can think of have operating expenses. Mutual funds are no different. An important thing to remember is that the mutual fund companies do not pay the ongoing operating expenses. You do!

The costs or operating expenses have profound consequences to the investor and consist of management or advisory fees, administrative fees and sometimes 12b-1 distribution fees. These expenses are deducted from the fund's assets, which is your money.

My favorite cost investors incur is the 12b-1 distribution fee. This is the expense you pay to have the fund company market, promote, advertise and distribute the fund to the public. What a great idea! Have you ever heard the term "using other people's money" to build a business. Of course you have. That is exactly what the fund companies are doing when they charge 12b-1 fees. So, the next time you see a slick commercial at half time of the Super Bowl or NBA championship game, promoting a specific mutual fund, remember it's your invested dollar paying for it. Bill Barker, in his article, "Expense Ratios" describes 12b-1 fees in this manner:

> If you're in a fund with a 12b-1 fee, you're paying every year for the fund to run commercials and try to sell itself. Can this in any way help you? Do you enjoy seeing advertisements of your fund or your fund family on television? Unless you really do, you should probably avoid funds that charge a 12b-1 fee.[12]

What a great business arrangement for the fund company. You pay for the promotion, which attracts new investors to the fund. The fund company then is able to produce more revenue for itself because its management fees are tied directly to fund size. I would think if a particular mutual fund is advertised and promoted to be such a great investment, then don't you think it appropriate for the fund company to pay for it and not you? I know one thing; if, in fact, I was invested in one of those rare funds with superior performance I certainly wouldn't want the whole world to know about it. Not only that, but the fund companies want me to pay to tell everyone on top of it. It's analogous to being a prospector during the Gold Rush in California and finding a rich vein of gold and placing a sign up saying, "Gold Found Here." Both seem to detract from my financial well being and ability to create wealth.

I mentioned earlier, while I was at Morgan Stanley Dean Witter, we used to have the middlemen from New York come visit us in Beverly Hills. The fund managers and analysts would speak to us about the merits of the particular fund they were running. It was usually an overview and followed by a question and answer session. These meetings usually lasted about an hour or so in the morning. Then the fund "operators" were many times off to a luncheon down the block at the Four Seasons Hotel, supposedly hosted by the firm, and open to the public. The meal usually consisted of a mixed green salad, rolls and butter and some sort of chicken dish followed by dessert. I will give the firm credit; there was no open bar and steak tartar was never served. Following the meal, the fund "operator" would lecture for about an hour with the objective of gaining the public's trust and hard-earned dollar. As I looked around the room at all the outsiders glued to the speaker, I smiled knowing it was them paying for the lunch—not the firm. Yet, they thought they were getting a good chicken meal for nothing.

Mutual funds, which have 12b-1 fees, range typically from .25% and all the way up to 1%. If we look at a medium sized fund with about $5 Billion in assets, a 12b-1 fee of .5% is no laughing matter. It means $25 million dollars of investors' hard-earned capital is being wasted annually on fund promotion. That's money no longer working for you as an investor. It's money, which has simply been flushed down the drain.

The big expense in mutual fund ownership is management fees. This is where the American public is being fleeced and for no good reason in order to richly line the pockets of the investment firms. It is how the mutual fund industry thrives, grows and prospers. It's in large measure how Wall Street can afford to pay the twenty-eight year old kid with a Harvard MBA $400,000 a year. The fee is the money "necessary" to pay the "manager" of the mutual fund. On average, this fee is about .5% to 1% annually of the fund's assets for large growth funds.

Part of the management fee does support the highly priced team of analysts and researchers who may travel the globe in order to visit companies to weed out good investments. What's not spent and kept in-house by the investment firms contributes substantially to their profits.

Management fees, 12b-1 fees and other administrative fund costs are usually grouped together and expressed as a ratio to fund asset size. That relationship, expressed as a percentage, is termed the "expense ratio." What's important in analyzing a fund's costs are not the individual expenses making up the expense ratio but rather the expense ratio itself. In this manner an investor can see on a relative basis how costly a particular fund is in comparison to others. Vanguard reports in its disclosure of the Vanguard U.S. Growth Fund dated May 1, 1999, that the average expense ratio for growth funds is 1.44%. By comparison, let's see how efficiently the ten largest equity funds operate as noted below.

Fund	$ Total Assets (In billions)	Expense Ratio %(*)	$ Taken from Investors
Magellan Fund	97.5	.60%	$585,000,000
Vanguard 500 Index	92.6	.18%	$166,680,000
Washington Mutual Inv.	58.6	.61%	$357,460,000
Investment Co. Of Am.	54.5	.55%	$299,750,000
Fidelity Growth & Inc.	50.5	.66%	$333,300,000
Fidelity ContraFund	43.5	.61%	$265,350,000
Vanguard Windsor II	35.2	.41%	$144,320,000
American Century Ultra	34.9	1.00%	$349,000,000
Janus Fund	32.3	.87%	$281,010,000
Vanguard Wellington	27.1	.31%	$ 84,010,000
Average of Funds Excluding Index Fund		.62%	

(*) Source: www. morningstar.com (September 30, 1999).

Why is it that the average growth fund has an expense ratio of 1.44% while the average of the nine largest actively managed funds is only .62%? The answer, in part, has to do with their fund size. It means fund costs do not increase in direct proportion to asset size. The idea is that the middlemen can just as easily and effectively manage a $50 billion fund as one 1/10th the size (I agree). The other factor is that smaller funds want to become bigger. In efforts to grow the asset base and become more profitable more (of your) money is spent on advertising and promotion. This is where the 12b-1 fees kick in at your expense. The larger the fund becomes the greater the management fee and hence the greater revenue and profitability to the firm.

The numbers are staggering if we look at the annual sums of money spent to "operate" the funds in our "behalf." The investment firms have taken an average of about $2,870,000,000 from us in those ten funds alone. I can't imagine it takes $2.87 billion annually to "properly" run those ten funds, can you? Yet, investors are silently handing over their money each year to the fund companies vis `a vis the ongoing operating expenses. If we look at the Magellan Fund, I've got to think that of the $585,000,000 spent by investors at least some of it must contribute to Fidelity's profit margin. As I see it, the real injustice is that the $2.87 billion, or so, spent annually is taken completely away from investors. It is money no longer able to compound and create wealth for you and me. For all intense and purposes the money has gone into the giant black hole in the sky.

According to David Harrell in his article entitled, "Funds of Funds" found at morningstar.com, he states: "Fund expenses are usually thought of (and measured) as a percentage of net assets, but they actually represent 10% to 20% of your expected long-term return."[13] The percentage being dependent upon the expense ratio. As noted before, a slightly smaller rate of return over many years proves to be quite substantial. The investing public through the costs of mutual fund ownership is losing vast sums of wealth. Just as your physical health deteriorates through cigarette smoking so, too, does your financial health suffer through paying management fees.

The average growth fund sports an expense ratio of 1.44%. Earlier we found the average return of growth funds to be 16.32% on an annualized basis inclusive of management fees over the last decade. Wouldn't it be nice if we could simply do away with fund expenses altogether or as much as possible?

You bet it would. For example, $10,000 invested today at a rate of return of 16.32% will be worth $45,300 in ten years, $205,600 in twenty years and $932,400 in thirty years. Conversely, if we could bypass the middleman all together, we could conceptually add another 1.44% to our return and become much wealthier by it. Ten thousand dollars invested today at a rate of 17.76% is worth $51,200 in ten years,

$263,000 in twenty years and $1,348,000 in thirty years. It seems unbelievable but the small rate of return differential of 1.44% can have huge consequences as to how you plan your retirement years. So, think twice before you put one nickel into a mutual fund (It could be one of the biggest mistakes you make in your life). There are investment alternatives we can all make which are much more cost effective. We can gain back most of the 1.44% lost to advertisements, promotions and fund management. Shortly I will give you some suggestions how.

How would you feel if long ago you invested in General Electric, IBM, Exxon or Ford and suddenly each company announced you'd only be paid 50% of your entitled dividends? Let's further complicate matters by saying you are retired and need the dividends to help support yourself. You'd been receiving a yield from those dividends of 3.5% and now your income is being cut by 50% to 1.75%. The answer is of course that you'd not be in the best of spirits.

In mutual fund investing a similar scenario exists. The only difference is that your income is sliced in half, or worse taken completely away, on day one of your investment. Mutual funds pay operating expenses (as in any business) out of revenue or gross income. The ongoing revenue stream for mutual funds are the dividends and interest income received from the investment portfolio. That's investors' money like yours and Cousin Jack and mine's being spent and lost for good. Based on review of the Magellan Fund Annual Report dated March 31, 1999, the fund reports total income of $952.7 million and expenses of $456 million. Therefore, about 48% of the fund's income has been taken away due to operating expenses. I'll be damned if I want half of my investment income taken away from me—just to be privileged of having my capital "properly invested."

Just how lucrative is the mutual fund industry? A few examples illustrate the point rather clearly.

Morgan Stanley Dean Witter in its 1998 Annual Report reports having 138 separate mutual funds with more than $121,000,000,000 ($121 billion) of invested funds from about three million investors. The firm reports having another $294 billion under management in its so-called Asset Management Group totaling $415 billion as of August 31, 1999.

CHART 8

Assets Under Management

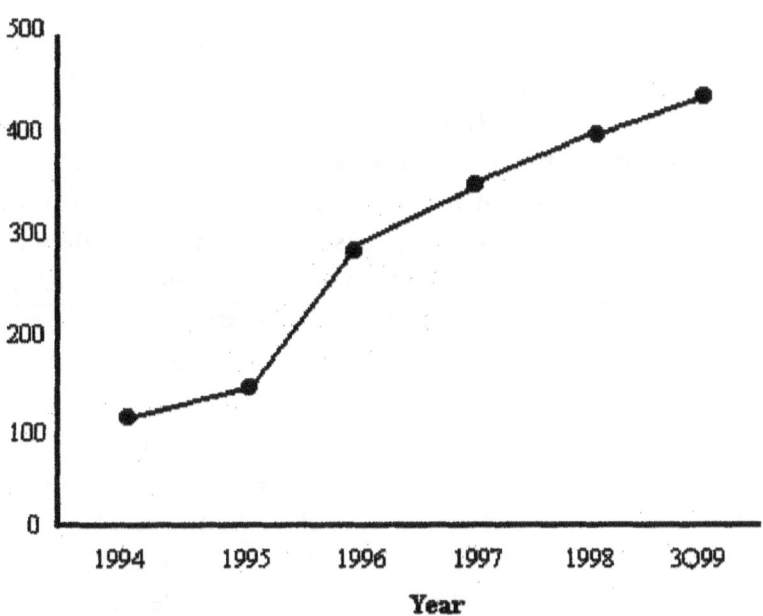

According to Morgan Stanley Dean Witter's Annual Report for 1998, its asset management, distribution and administrative fees were $2.848 billion on $376 billion under management for the prior year. That represents a fee a shade over .75% payable to the firm for dollars under management. The firm further reports its total operating expenses to be $5.7 billion. It means roughly 50 % of the firm's entire operating expenses are covered each January 1st through its derived management fees alone. That's because as Chairman Phil Purcell's states in a letter to shareholders, "Asset management...tends to produce steady revenue streams."[14] It's money that can be counted on year after year as long as strong investor demand continues. Almost everything else the firm does during the year is gravy and adds directly to bottom line profit—including, trading, commissions, lending and investment banking services.

Fidelity Investments reports at its web site during October 1999 that it " has grown to become America's largest privately held investment manager with more than $1 trillion in customer assets."[15] As of October 1999, Fidelity had ninety-five equity funds alone. Recently I've written to the US Treasury Department for my courtesy copy of Fidelity's tax return. I have yet to receive a copy. Because Fidelity is a privately held corporation (unlike Morgan Stanley Dean Witter or Merrill Lynch), we can only estimate revenues generated from its investment management activities. Fidelity's funds do tend to have lower expense ratios than funds managed by Morgan Stanley Dean Witter. If Fidelity receives .5% (instead of MSDW's .75%) on average for all its managed funds (bond and money market funds tend to have much lower expense ratios), then with $1 trillion dollars under management the revenue can be figured at about $5 billion annually. No matter how you slice it $5 billion is a lot of money coming out of investors' pockets. No wonder its President Edward C. Johnson III and daughter Abigail are two of the richest in America and are members of the Forbes 400 list. According to the October 11, 1999 issue that lists the 400 wealthiest citizens—these two had an estimated net worth of $11.1 billion!

I've just mentioned two fund families—Morgan Stanley Dean Witter and Fidelity. There are many others in the industry and probably at least one for each letter of the alphabet. There are now in the neighborhood of 7,000 mutual funds. You can envision why the dollars generated in behalf of the mutual fund industry, through its fee arrangement, is quite extraordinary. I imagine they have a powerful group of lobbyists in Washington. With all this financial clout, it's no wonder the media treats the mutual fund industry like a delicate flower.

Another few words about fund management. When you invest in the average mutual fund, about 8% of your invested dollar remain in cash. Management fees are calculated on total fund size not total fund size less the sums of money held in cash. Therefore, you as an investor are being charged 1.44% on average by the fund to simply hold your cash. Throughout the years cash has provided about a 4% return. But through mutual fund ownership your typical return is reduced to 2.56%. So, if you want to keep cash lying around (and you probably should for safety reasons), you can see why it's best to simply purchase a certificate of deposit at your local bank.

Over the last few years there has been a lot of discussion in the media about how best to pick a mutual fund for investment. One of the key notions is to find the best fund manager you can—meaning the one that's beaten the index most frequently and by the highest percentage. Once you've found that special person, regardless of the fund currently being managed, he or she dictates the fund you invest in.

The problem with this course of action is that fund managers are human beings. A "hot" manager one-year may "cool" the next and then achieve only average performance. They are just like anyone else who goes through the highs and lows in life. In addition, their lives are subject to alteration at any time. They don't need to give you prior notice of impending change. Just as you've probably changed positions or careers in the workforce, so do fund managers. It happens all the time in the mutual fund industry. The fund manager you thought you were hiring to invest and "manage" your funds may easily leap to another firm for the almighty dollar, being closer to home, to spend more time with the kids, or any number of other reasons. Any fund manager is very unlikely to be in control of your funds for greater than five years. So what happens is the "red hot" manager (you researched for and ultimately hired) departs and another one arrives to take his or her place. Yet, your dollar usually remains invested in the fund. Given today's work environment you are probably more apt to have an encounter with an extraterrestrial (ET) than to meet a fund manager who has been at the helm for thirty years.

A perfect example of this is the Fidelity Magellan fund where investors flocked to invest with the legendary Peter Lynch. Mr. Lynch ran Magellan for thirteen years and during that time his fund pulverized the S & P 500 in gaining a little more than 2,700% to about 500% for the index. Then Peter Lynch moved on in 1992 and Jeffrey Vinik was hired to replace him. Mr. Vinik's performance was no better than sub par, and in 1996, only four years after being promoted to run the largest mutual fund in America, he "resigned." In comes another fund manager. Now it's Robert Stansky's turn in 1996 and he has been at the helm since that time. The amazing fact is that with all this turmoil at the fund, its size actually grew from about $22 billion in 1992 at the time of Mr. Lynch's departure to over $97.5 billion in 1999. Yes, part of this has to do with the market rising dramatically during this period. But another reason has been the continued influx of cash from investors even though the fund has performed only marginally at best since Mr. Lynch's departure.

Patricia Dunn, Chairman of Barclays Global Investors was interviewed in the October 1999 issue of Money magazine. The interviewer asks her, "If index funds outperform the average actively managed fund, why are active funds so popular?" Her answer, "A cosmic question! I believe it has a lot to do with a yearning that people have to identify individual geniuses who can beat everybody else when it comes to investing..." The interviewer continues by asking, "How do we explain a fund such as Bill Miller's Legg Mason Value Trust, which has bested the S & P 500 for eight years?" She responds, "It may be luck. It may be skill. It's not my belief that there's no such thing as genius when it comes to investing. But there are very, very few geniuses, and the problem is that no one's ever come up with a reliable way to identify those managers in advance."[16]

I love the game of baseball. I take my son who is now almost five to see the Dodgers and Angels on a fairly regular basis. Matthew has taken a fond liking to the game and his favorite thing to do is play catch with me. In baseball, a career .300 hitter is revered and he can usually be found in the hall of fame. Babe Ruth, Ted Williams and Joe DiMaggio did it just to name a few. Ty Cobb, who was probably the greatest hitter of all time, had a lifetime average of .366. I equate the solid and steady performance of the S & P 500 to being a .300 hitter (exceptionally hard to do better than consistently). I believe investors trying to find the greatest manager or "hitter of all time" waste a lot of unnecessary energy (or scouting). It's tough enough for a professional full time scout to find that special .300 hitter wherever he may be growing up—in Cuba, a farm in Ohio or the streets of New York. But for a part-time novice investor to ferret out the next Peter Lynch seems highly unlikely. It seems much more efficient to me to simply invest in the index and have hall of fame returns. There has been only one .350 hitter in the mutual fund industry the last eight years who has consistently beaten the index. It has probably much more due to luck than skill to have invested with Bill Miller at Legg Mason. So, if you're intent on owning a mutual fund, I suggest you look at an index fund rather than trying to locate the next "Ty Cobb" of fund managers.

You can guess by now I was not the top mutual fund salesperson at Dean Witter. The big line drilled into brokers' heads within the firm was and is still, "Do what's right" (denoting Dean Witter Reynolds) for the client. I never felt mutual funds were worthwhile for any of my clients. I felt a strong moral obligation to them. I didn't want the investment firms and the Harvard MBA's they hire to prosper at my clients' expense. In many respects I believe the mutual fund industry is nothing short of legalized larceny. I hope by now you concur to some degree.

There is one thing we as investors can do to stop the fleecing by the mutual fund industry. We don't have to follow Peter Finch's advice in the movie *Network* on how to have things changed when he expounds, "My life has value! So I want you to get up now. I want all of you to get up out of your chairs. I want you to get up right now and go to the window, open it, and stick your head out, and yell, **I'm as mad as hell, and I'm not going to take this anymore...** Things have got to change." We can get the same message across by simply making a conscientious effort to stop investing in mutual funds.

A very close friend of mine, one who I have known since my sandlot days growing up in Cleveland, Ohio works for Morgan Stanley Dean Witter. He has built his business and reputation by only selling tax-free municipal bonds to clients. I applaud him for this. I believe this is the most ethical way to make a living in the securities business. John believes as I do, that if there is more than one adjective associated with an investment you should probably stay away from it. Terms like "cumulative convertible preferred stock," "subordinated 8% debentures," "short term trust," and (my favorite), "master limited partnership" typically only benefit the issuer and its agent and not the investor (Again the notion of, if they're selling.. I probably shouldn't be buying). I've never heard of anyone creating substantial wealth for themselves in any of these Wall Street-sponsored investments. But I've heard and read many stories where investors lost their shirts. Yet, each week hundreds of investments with a lot of adjectives are brought to the market for the investor to be suckered into and screwed. If you have a decent memory you may recall the huge problems Prudential Securities faced from investor lawsuits in the early 1990s concerning its sponsored limited partnerships. These were investments heavily promoted by Prudential as being both sound and secure. Well things didn't turn out that way. Prudential later settled the various lawsuits by paying back billions of dollars to investors. The firm suffered much more so by losing credibility and a lot of clients and brokers to other investment houses.

Let's discuss several other investment "opportunities" besides mutual funds which also takes advantage of investors.

One of the more popular investment strategies for conservative long-term growth is the "Dogs of the Dow" approach. This method of investing was clearly outlined in Michael O'Higgins book entitled, *Beating The Dow*. The strategy is a simple one, whereby an investor buys in equal dollar amounts the ten Dow stocks with the highest current yield (from dividends) and holds this group for one year. After the year is up, those stocks no longer in the top ten are sold and then replaced by the new stocks which have entered the top ten. Your portfolio consists of these ten stocks and that's it. The investment is not a mutual fund because your funds aren't actively managed. There are no management fees. The theory behind this sound strategy is that the ten stocks yielding the most are depressed and out of favor in the market. You are supposedly buying very strong and highly capitalized companies at good prices and are being paid handsomely to be patient. Dividends produce about 30% of an investor's total return in stocks. So, receipt of the dividends is nothing to sneeze at. The current list of the "Dogs of the Dow" is as follows as of December 31, 1999.

Company	Yield	Price	
Philip Morris	8.10%	$ 24	*
JP Morgan	3.16%	$127	
Caterpillar	2.83%	$ 46	*
GM	2.75%	$ 73	
Eastman Kodak	2.69%	$ 65	
MMM	2.32%	$ 96	
Exxon Mobil	2.19%	$ 80	
DuPont	2.15%	$ 65	*
SBC Communications	2.04%	$ 48	*
International Paper	1.83%	$ 54	*

Yields and prices are reflected as of December 31, 1999

This method of investing has produced superior returns to most mutual funds and the index itself for at least a quarter of a century. According to information obtained at motleyfool.com, the compounded average growth rate of the "Dogs of the Dow," was 17.95% for the twenty-five year period from 1974—1998 compared with 14.40% for the Dow Jones Average. The ten-year period from 1989—1998 produced slightly lower returns for the "Dogs" at 17.22%. We know most mutual funds underperform the index.

There are several other variations to the ten-stock approach. Another popular method of investing is the "Select 5" or buying the five lowest-priced of the ten highest dividend-yielding stocks in the Dow Jones Industrial Average. Hold these stocks for a year and then make adjustments accordingly year after year. You have five stocks in your portfolio and that's it. This method is so simple and mechanical. It doesn't require you to hire a Harvard MBA to guide you. The current five are indicated above by an (*). The "Select Five" strategy according to motleyfool.com has far surpassed the performance of the index too. During a comparable twenty-five year period, the five-stock approach's annualized return was 19.25%—even higher than the ten-stock method. Over the ten-year period ending 1998 the returns measured 18.07% again slightly superior to the "Dogs" return. The average mutual fund if you recall returned 16.58% for the ten-year period ending March 1999, according to Fidelity Investments.

Both of these investments, the top-ten or the low-five, are time tested and proven over many years to be fairly worthwhile. Many brokerage houses (including Morgan Stanley Dean Witter, Merrill Lynch and Painewebber) offer these two investments to the public in two ways: direct stock ownership or through ownership in a unit investment trust. Let's say you have $25,000 to invest. In the first method, you would simply call your broker and he or she would buy $2,500 worth of each of the ten stocks or $5,000 worth of five stocks for you. Initially these stocks are owned proportionately; each representing 10% or 20% of the portfolio. When the year is up you and your broker review the portfolio and make the necessary buy/sell decisions to follow the strategy.

There are two ways your portfolio changes from year to year. First, there are infrequent additions and deletions to the Dow Jones Average (Earlier I presented the most recent changes to the index.). If you own a certain stock in your portfolio and it ceases to be part of the index, then you are supposed to remove the stock from your holdings. Second, a stock in your portfolio can rise enough in value during the year whereby it no longer supports one of the ten highest yields. Let's compare today's "dogs" with the "dogs" of yesteryear. The ten stocks sporting the highest yields as of September 1, 1991 were as follows:

Company	Yield	Price
Westinghouse	5.80%	$ 24
IBM	5.10%	$ 97
Texaco	5.00%	$ 64
Sears	4.70%	$ 42
Allied-Signal	4.60%	$ 39
Chevron	4.60%	$ 72
Union Carbide	4.60%	$ 22
Eastman Kodak	4.50%	$ 43
Exxon	4.50%	$ 58
GM	4.10%	$ 38

Source: *The Wall Street Journal,* 1 September 1991

It's interesting to note that Kodak, GM and Exxon (now Exxon Mobil) appear on both lists (1991 and 1999). However, they may not have been part of the "Dogs" in the years in between. Since 1991, Chevron, Sears, Texaco, Union Carbide and Westinghouse have been removed from the index so they are disqualified from being part of the

"Dogs" in 2000—even though each may still have attractive yields. Allied Signal and IBM have risen enough in value since 1991 to no longer qualify in 1999 (at year end) to be christened a "Dog"—even though the two remain part of the index. Additionally, certain Dow stocks are rarely found to be a "Dog." Stocks like Coca-Cola, Hewlett-Packard, Intel, Microsoft and McDonalds have low dividend payout policies, whereby they retain a majority of earnings for future growth rather than paying shareholders back in the form of dividends. Another certainty in life is: we can "never say never" and there may come a time when these stocks are transformed into "Dogs." Just look at what's happened to Philip Morris since 1991. The stock wasn't even measured to be a "Dog" in 1991 and since that time with all the tobacco litigation surrounding the industry and the company it's now "Dog" number 1— sporting a hefty dividend yield over 8%.

Over the course of a year, about two to three stocks become part of the top ten. This means you are adding and subtracting about 2 ½ stocks from the portfolio annually. In other words, your turnover rate in following the strategy is about 25% year in and year out. This figure is quite a bit lower than the normal 85% rate for mutual funds but it's about five times higher than an S & P 500 index fund. The good news for you in following this direct ownership strategy is your after-tax returns are closer to your pretax returns than with the typical mutual fund.

Unfortunately, your direct ownership in the five or ten stocks does come with costs. When you buy the portfolio from your broker you of course have up front commissions to pay. Next, are the annual commissions you are forced to pay as you follow the strategy. Year after year, you have roughly two to three buy orders and the same number of sell orders executed by your broker. These commissions can add up significantly. Brokers love this business because it can usually be counted on each year. It tends to be an annuity of commissions for them. Your other costs, which brokers don't like to mention, are the annual capital gains tax you may be forced to pay Uncle Sam. Remember anytime you buy and later sell anything for a profit, Uncle Sam has his hand out waiting. All these costs add up over time and to your detriment! I think you get the picture that if you had actually invested in the "Dogs of the Dow" in 1974 your real return would have been a lot lower than 17.95% through 1998.

The second method of investing in the "Dogs" is through ownership of a unit investment trust—brought to you courtesy of the middlemen on Wall Street. A unit trust is like a mutual fund except there are no management fees. Investors purchase and own units (or shares) of the trust. The trust, in turn, owns the stocks. A trustee is appointed and overseas the duties and responsibilities assigned to it vis-à-vis a trust agreement. Trustees of unit investment trusts do not make investment decisions, which is the big difference between mutual funds and its managers. Because of this "hands off" approach, the ongoing costs of unit trusts are usually much lower than mutual funds. For example, Morgan Stanley Dean Witter's Select Equity Trust has a projected total operating expense of a mere .125% (of assets) as found in the prospectus dated July 1, 1999. This is a far cry lower than the average mutual fund, which sports an expense ratio of 1.44%. Does this mean we, as investors, should dump all of our hard-earned money into any kind of unit investment trust and forget mutual funds? Hardly. Unit trusts (like the top-ten or low- five) take advantage of investors in other ways. Unit trusts are "packaged products" sponsored by the investment houses—just like mutual funds. Again, I repeat—anything, which comes with fancy pictures, graphs and descriptions to entice you to invest, comes at your expense. Some of the brochures I've seen regarding the top-ten or low-five distributed by the various firms can get pretty sexy. Wall Street is packaging these simple strategies into unit investment trusts and getting rich at your expense in the process.

Morgan Stanley Dean Witter rewards itself in the following manner from investors in the trust:

Sales Charge

Amount Invested	Percent of Public Offering Price
Less than $25,000	2.90%
$25,000 to 49,999	2.75%
$50,000 to 99,999	2.50%
$100,000 to 249,999	2.25%
$250,000 to 999,999	2.00%
$1,000,000 or more	1.00%
Exchanges (Rollovers)	2.00%

Source:Morgan Stanley Dean Witter Select Equity Trust prospectus 1 July 1999.

The more you invest the lower is your commission rate and rightfully so. However, the small first-time investor, who is trying to create a nest egg for him or herself, is the one penalized the most (up to 2.90% of their invested funds). Nobody ever said life was fair.

The real problem with the Dow-ten or Dow-five trusts come later on as investors are exposed to annual rollover charges. The trusts are set up to have maturity dates one year later. When the trust expires in a years time investors have the right to "rollover" their invested funds into next year's trust. No matter what dollars were invested initially, investors are charged 2% annually to continue in the investment for successive years. That, my friend, is how Wall Street makes big money off you and me. The annual 2% charge is quite a bit higher than the average mutual fund's expense ratio of 1.44%. So, the reported return of the "Dogs of the Dow" of 17.95% over the last twenty-five years or so can be shaved at least 2% for those invested in the trust program since 1974. Now we're down to a 15.95% return, which comes closer to the Dow Jones Average return of 14.40% during the same period. I don't have to illustrate again the wealth investors could have left on the table by forfeiting this 2% annualized return. Over a twenty-five year period the number is huge, as we know—even on a $10,000 investment. Again Wall Street has created a program to prosper off the unsuspecting and naive investor.

The situation worsens for investors if the unit trust investment is held outside of a tax deferred account. As stocks in the trust appreciate, so does the value of the trust. At the end of each year the trust matures. This is a big drawback to these investments because it usually forces investors to pay capital gains tax. If investors continue in the unit trust strategy year after year, there will be ongoing tax payments. Because investors are forced to pay Uncle Sam its bounty, the true or after-tax rate of return is lowered. For example, if the UIT provided investors with a pretax return of 15.95% from 1974—1998, we can be reasonably assured 10% of the return or 1.595% needs to be subtracted to find the after-tax return (Remember earlier, the average mutual fund has a 14% adjustment factor). Now the twenty-five year performance is down to about 14.35% when viewed, and, as it should be, on an after-tax basis. A darn good investment return of 17.95% has been whittled down to 14.35%; thanks to the middlemen and the US Treasury Department.

Be wary of any "packaged product" sponsored by Wall Street—including mutual funds and unit investment trusts. The costs of each will usually seriously detract from your ability to create wealth over time. If you ever have the urge to invest in the "Dogs of the Dow" then by all means avoid investing in the unit investment trust and invest yourself. I'd like to add a new twist to the strategy:

Once you've purchased the ten stocks from your broker don't call him or her back for about thirty years to review. No trades—nothing! I have a dear friend, Lance, and, as he used to say to clients, "The only decision you really need to make " Mrs. Bugelman" is what time of day in thirty years are you planning on calling back—morning or afternoon. Either is available right now." Needless to say, Lance is no longer in the securities business either. If investors followed this approach, there would be no ongoing commissions or capital gains tax payments to make. I venture this approach will create more wealth for investors than the current Dow strategy in place. Only time will tell. I guarantee one thing however. You won't find an investment firm sponsoring and promoting this strategy. All that's needed is for the top-ten or low-five trusts to have thirty-year maturity dates as opposed to one. This would end the 2% annual payments to Wall Street. It would end the promotions to attract other investors with your dollar. It would also make it unprofitable (or not profitable enough) for the investment firms to involve themselves. And that's why it won't happen.

The latest craze on Wall Street with a fancy name (and a few too many adjectives) is professional money management. This is another way the middleman siphon's off your hard-earned dollar.

Let's say you have recently come into an inheritance of $100,000 from your recently departed grandmother. You've heard from friends and other family members that it might be a wise idea to hire a professional money manager. Your next call is to your broker with whom you have a few bucks socked away. You tell him or her your story and then you are invited to the office at the broker's suggestion. You are offered and given a cup of coffee and have your parking ticket validated. Next, the broker pulls out a questionnaire for you to complete in about ten minutes. The form has about four boxes on top and you are supposed to check one of them. Each small box represents the investment objective you are seeking. Depending on your age, risk tolerance and a few other factors, you determine and check the box most appropriate for you. It might be conservation of capital through bond investing. It might be balanced growth through a portfolio both bonds and stocks. Let's say you check the box for growth through capital appreciation. You then complete the form and the broker says, "I'll get back to you in a few days and thanks for dropping by." Next week your broker calls back with a few recommendations. He or she has found a few "very good" money managers available for hire given your investment desires. The list usually includes a money manager within the firm (say your broker is with Merrill Lynch) and several others. You make the call who's best for you and maybe the broker assists you. You've now hired a professional money manager. In a few weeks time, the money manager, who takes care of all investment decisions for you, assembles a portfolio of stocks with your $100,000. Now all you do is just sit back and relax and let nature take its course. That's a big mistake!!

A money manager is nothing more than a mutual fund manager hired by you on a micro level. You own the stocks picked by the money manager outright rather than "pooled" with other investors in a mutual fund. The money manager comes with the education from Harvard (which you don't need) and a hefty price tag (which you don't need either). Brokers and investment houses like to have clients enrolled in money management programs because, as with mutual funds, these create annual annuities of commissions and fees. Brokers can sleep better at night because they know where their next dollar is coming from as they are rewarded continually for assets under management. As the assets rise in value, and new clients enroll in asset management, so too, does the agent's income. The perception in the marketplace is that your broker is your ally because he or she is not working on a transactional commission basis. The broker doesn't have to pick up the phone and call "Dr. Schwartz" and sell him 200 shares of General Electric to make a fee. Rather you and your broker are a team working together in pursuit of your best interests. But, remember what's usually good for Wall Street is usually bad for you.

The compensation you pay Wall Street varies only slightly from one firm to the next. Morgan Stanley Dean Witter represents its money management or "Access" fee schedule for equity portfolios to be the following as of October 30, 1999:

Asset Level	Fee
First $500,000	3.00%
Next $500,000	2.50%
On next $1,000,000	2.00%
On assets over $2,000,000	1.60%

Source: www.msdw.com (November 1, 1999).

Some firms may charge lower fees, but be careful because they may charge commissions on top of the lower fee arrangement. It's apparent most investors will fall into the first category above and be charged 3% of assets under management. How hefty a price tag! If Wall Street could charge more, they probably would. If you recall the average mutual fund charges 1.44%, and that's expensive. It means forfeiting 3% of your annual return to compensate the Harvard MBA. Why should you pay the twenty-eight year old kid on Wall Street 3% a year to pick stocks like Intel, Microsoft, General Electric, Merck and Exxon—something you could do just as easily yourself? The answer of course is you shouldn't.

Additionally, on top of the 3% you are paying, you may also be forced to pay capital gains tax resulting from trades the money manager deems necessary to alter the portfolio in your best interest. Sound familiar to a mutual fund? This of course reduces your real or true rate of return even further.

The situation worsens for you if you've accumulated $100,000 worth of stock and decide to place it with a money manager. Let's say you were smart enough to put money aside throughout the years and bought high quality big name stocks. The cost basis on some of your stocks may be next to nothing. The dividends you now receive may be twenty, thirty, and forty percent or even higher of your original invested funds. Owning stocks like General Electric, Philip Morris, First Union, and Glaxo Holdings (from my own experiences) can do this sort of thing. But, the money manager has quote "better ideas for you." Not only do you immediately turn over 3% of your return by signing on the dotted line; you've also given the manager the power to decide and trade. Watch out—because in order to justify his or her existence (and the 3% fee), the manager won't idly sit by. Watch as your Philip Morris stock is sold and your 20% return on cost blows up in smoke and you are forced to pay about 1/3 of your profits to Uncle Sam. Or watch as the General Electric stock you've held for twenty years, which has performed so well, is suddenly pared back and sold by the manager because he or she was simply following the twenty-eight year old analyst's opinion. The actions by the money managers in these cases are unjustifiable but do happen.

Be wary the next time a relative passes away and you inherit $100,000. Don't listen to friends and relatives about the merits of hiring a money manager. In so doing, it may be one of the biggest mistakes you make in your life.

PART 2

What it's Okay to Do

Okay, so investing in mutual funds, certain unit investment trusts and hiring money managers is not a good idea. What's left? What can you do to help yourself? The next part of the book will hopefully give you the guidance you need so that you can reach your dreams and not be taken advantage of unnecessarily.

Let's say you are a busy individual. You are working ten hours a day to support a family—with a spouse and two children. Or you are a single parent, working and trying to raise three children at home and you don't have the time or inclination to follow the stock market. Maybe you have no experience in investments and when you hear the term "CD" you think compact disc rather than certificate of deposit. If this sounds like you, then there are investments you can make which require little time, effort and energy on your part. If history means anything, you'll probably do much better for yourself, financially, than your neighbor across the street who has chosen mutual funds.

If you haven't guessed by now, I'm alluding to indexed investments. In contrast to mutual funds your hard-earned capital is almost fully invested—working for you. The costs are cheap and Wall Street firms won't be getting rich off of you either. Most of all 85% or so of all mutual funds underperform the index anyway. Therefore, if you are a novice investor or you don't have the time, desire and inclination to study investments then adopt the words "if you can't beat 'em join 'em."

The investment world has created silly little names like "spiders," "diamonds," and "webs" to reference these simple yet powerful investments. Today, there are many indices created by man to judge stock performance. The S & P 500 and the Dow Jones Industrial Average are two of course. There is the S & P MidCap 400, which seeks to measure the performance of smaller domestic companies. Or, the NASDQ-100 which judges the largest non-financial companies on the NASDAQ Stock Market. There is the important Morgan Stanley Capital International Indexes set up to evaluate market performances mainly overseas. At the end of October 1999 there existed fifty-four separate indexes created by Morgan Stanley to judge the various developed markets. The list can go on and on.

Earlier, we showed it doesn't pay to own too much. All you need is a few investments (three or so indexed investments) and you should be more than amply diversified. The important point for investors with little time, interest or energy to do anything more than index investing is to develop a savings plan, stick to it and start as early in life as possible. Index investors should do—rather than think. Chart 10 depicts how your annualized return would have been affected if you were lucky enough to have invested $10,000 annually from 1989—1998 at the market's low point vs. investing in the market at its annual peak:

CHART 9

If you had invested $10,000 on the "best" day—the day that the market hit its low for the year—here's how your investment would look				If you had invested $10,000 on the "worst" day—the day that the market hit its high for the year—here's how your investment would look		
Market low	**Cumulative investment**	**Year-end account value***		**Market high**	**Cumulative investment**	**Year-end account value***
1/3/89	$10,000	$13,274		10/9/89	$10,000	$9,902
10/11/90	$20,000	$24,143		7/16/90	$20,000	$18,717
1/9/91	$30,000	$45,284		12/31/91	$30,000	$34,394
4/8/92	$40,000	$60,025		12/18/92	$40,000	$46,954
1/8/93	$50,000	$77,222		12/28/93	$50,000	$61,635
4/4/94	$60,000	$88,966		2/2/94	$60,000	$72,281
1/3/95	$70,000	$136,029		12/13/95	$70,000	$109,311
1/10/96	$80,000	$179,828		11/25/96	$80,000	$144,177
1/2/97	$90,000	$253,137		12/5/97	$90,000	$202,115
1/9/98	$100,000	$338,777		12/29/98	$100,000	$269,691
Result: The average annual total return would have been 22.44%				*Result:* The average annual total return would have been 20.39%		

**The S&P 500 Index, is an unmanaged index generally considered to be representative of general stock market activity. Please note that indices do not take into account any fees and expenses of individual securities that they track, and that individuals cannot invest directly in any index. Data about the performance of this index are prepared or obtained by Neuberger Berman Management,Inc. and include reinvestment of all dividends and capital gain distribution.

Source: Reprinted, by permission of Neuberger and Berman

The results from above point out something very noteworthy. Being extremely lucky and investing on the "best day" of each year provided only a shade better than a 2% annualized return than being extremely unfortunate and investing on the "worst day" of each year. No one is apt to do either. An investor probably has a better chance of walking down the street to the nearest Seven-Eleven store and buying a $2 dollar lottery ticket and winning $2.5 million than he does or she does in guessing and investing in the market at its annual low ten years consecutively. Investors' trying to time the market for a "bottom" is an exercise in futility. However, delaying your entry into the market for years on end is very costly. Even if you had invested on the "worst day" of each year for the ten-year period, your annualized return would have been 20.39% compared to retaining cash and maybe earning 4%. The moral being—take action, pick out a few index investments (it takes about twenty minutes) invest, fasten your seat belt and enjoy the ride. Let's take a closer look at a few index investments and see why "spiders," "diamonds," and "webs" are gaining so much in popularity.

Indexing is not a new concept. One of the largest mutual funds in existence is the Vanguard 500 index fund—designed to track the performance of the S & P 500. The expense ratio is a meager .18% because there is not much to decide upon. No worldwide travel is needed or expended to find investments. The fund manager is not actively trying to spend your money with no benefit to you. The investor gets a piece of 500 designated stocks and that's it. With a meager 6% turnover rate you are not penalized terribly by Uncle Sam either. The returns, no matter how they are judged, beat almost all managed funds. A similar investment you may wish to consider is a "spider."

The American Stock Exchange first introduced the trading of SPDRs or "spiders" about six or seven years ago. "Spiders" are exchange traded unit investment trusts. There are many different "species" of them now in existence. The first one created was a unit investment trust based upon the companies in the S & P 500. This particular unit investment trust holds all the companies in the S & P 500. Investors simply buy shares or "units" just like a stock. The SPDR trust trades on the AMEX under the symbol SPY. Just like the Vanguard index fund, your returns are designed to mirror the S & P 500. If you think I'm kidding then look at Chart 10.

CHART 10

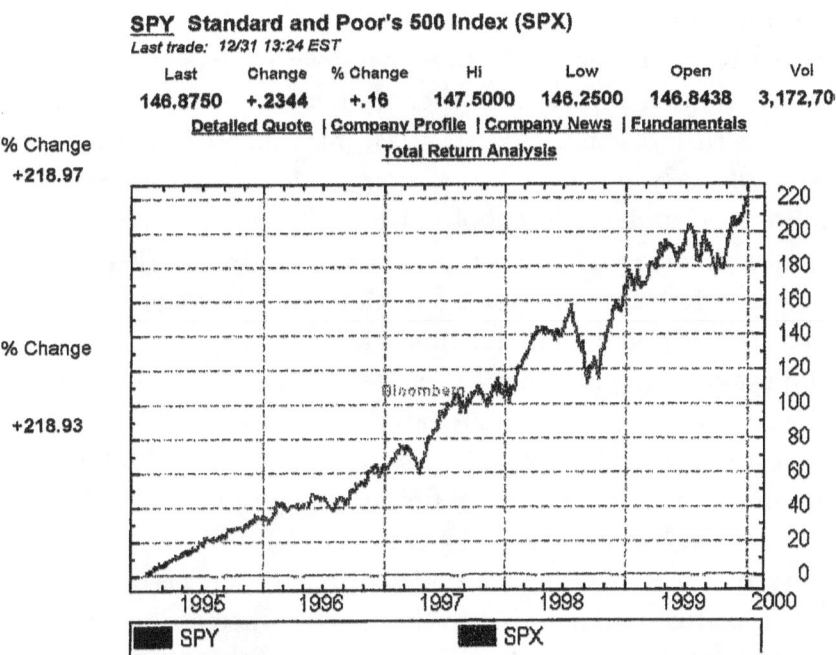

SPY Standard and Poor's 500 Index (SPX)
Last trade: 12/31 13:24 EST

Last	Change	% Change	Hi	Low	Open	Vol
146.8750	+.2344	+.16	147.5000	146.2500	146.8438	3,172,70

Detailed Quote | Company Profile | Company News | Fundamentals

Total Return Analysis

% Change
+218.97

% Change

+218.93

SPY   SPX

Source: Reprinted, by permission of Bloomberg L.P.

The return of the "spider" is going to be slightly less than the index itself because of trading costs and expenses. This is depicted in the graph where over the five-year period ending December 31, 1999 the S & P 500 provided a total return of 218.97% vs. 218.93% for "spider." It's as close as you can get to match the performance of the index.

The costs, expenses and turnover rates of the "spider" are nearly identical to the Vanguard fund. The only major difference between the two is how they are legally structured and traded which has no bearing on your rate of return.

There are two important reasons that give "spiders" a big advantage over most mutual funds and other unit investment trusts—like the Dow ten earlier discussed. First, as we have described most mutual funds hold cash positions—the average being about 8% of the portfolio. The "spiders" don't hold cash at all. One hundred per cent of the hard-earned capital you wanted invested in the market is invested and working for you. You don't face the situation where 8% of your invested funds is potentially earning a much lower rate of return. You have no catch up to play with the market as you do with mutual funds. If an investor needs cash he or she can easily sell shares on the exchange. The investor is simply cashed out by the buyer and the buyer takes ownership of the units. A mutual fund on the other hand redeems in a more archaic fashion—by holding cash.

The second reason giving SPDRs such an advantage is the fact it is set up with a maturity date well into the future, whereas the High-ten or Low-five trusts mature annually. Upon review of the SPDR Trust, Series 1 prospectus dated January 25, 1999, the termination date of the Trust is derived from a complicated mathematical exercise based upon a series of events and dates. It may mature in 2118 or 125 years from the date of inception. Let's just say for most of us unless we move to France and go on a strict yogurt diet the Trust will continue to exist in our lifetime. Because of the extended maturity date, investors in the "spider" aren't forced to pay annual capital gains tax based upon the appreciated value of the Trust's shares. So, if the "spider" went up 20% for the year, you wouldn't be required to send Uncle Sam roughly 1/3 of your gain as you might with the other unit trust strategies. The capital you are able to retain remains invested, compounding for you in the future. Again, a key ingredient to wealth creation is keeping as much money in your pocket after-tax and have it compound at the highest rate possible. By comparison, the Dow-ten unit trust falls far short. Its annual maturity usually forces you to send Uncle Sam a large percentage of your profits. The payments, of course, result in a much lower true rate of return than otherwise (unless you hold the trust in a tax-deferred account).

"Spiders" are very efficient investments because turnover, costs and tax payments are kept to a minimum. Just how efficient? Given the "spider" has costs of about .2% and a turnover rate of 6% annually, the impact this has on deriving the after-tax return is negligible. Earlier we showed a 6% turnover rate reduces the rate of return only 1% of the pretax return. If the S & P 500 returned 18.21% over the last ten years, then reductions of .1821% and .2% from the return or .38% has little impact on the investor compared to reductions the average mutual fund faces of 2.28%. A 17.8% return on an after-tax basis for the last ten years is certainly a lot better than 14%, which the average fund reported. I'll take the former. I trust you'd do the same. A great alternative for investors is to buy and hold "spider" or the Vanguard 500 and forget that actively managed mutual funds even exist.

With the growth and popularity of the SPDRs Trust, The American Stock Exchange in early 1998, launched the trading of the DIAMONDS Trust which seeks to mirror the performance of the all- important Dow Jones Industrial Average. The mechanics are the same for an investor as with "spider." Once again you buy "units" or shares traded on the exchange. Only this time the trading symbol is DIA and your ownership interest of the long-term unit investment trust gives you immediate exposure to the stocks comprising the Dow. Once again, the

DIAMONDS Trust is not actively managed. With the absence of management fees and high costs the investment is anticipated to be another very efficient investment. All other benefits with "spider" come along with this one as well—namely the high percentage of invested funds, very long maturation, low turnover, low tax payments and excellent historical performance.

The only time turnover occurs in the unit trust is when there is a change in composition of the Dow Jones Industrial Average. In the last three or so years there have been eight stocks replaced in the thirty stock index. However, from the period 1976—1996 only eleven total changes occurred. This equates to a exceedingly low turnover rate of just under 3% for the twenty-three year period ending 1999. Turnover, of course can potentially have a negative impact on investors as they may be forced to pay capital gains tax. The very low turnover rate of 3% associated with "DIAMONDS" may give it a slight edge in efficiency even over the SPDR Trust with its historic 6% rate.

We must recall both the S & P 500 and the Dow Jones Industrial Average have performed almost identically throughout the years. So, it's okay to invest in one or the other or both. Don't give in to mutual fund advertisements and endorsements so easily. Take ten minutes and order a trust prospectus to learn more about these indexed investments. Call your broker or the American Stock Exchange directly at (800) The AMEX and tell them Ted sent you. Since it's impractical to buy thirty stocks outright and recreate the weighted averaging of stocks in the index let the DIAMONDS Trust do this for you. The Trust has and will in all likelihood continue to vastly outperform most equity mutual funds worth consideration. Let's start by taking some of our hard-earned capital, by keeping it away from the middleman, and putting it in investments which have historically performed much better.

So far in this book there has been quite a bit of discussion about "the market" and "market performance." I've been referring all along to large capitalized companies located here in the US and the two most popular indexes—namely the Dow Jones Industrial Average and the Standard & Poors 500. However, for periods of time this big-firm, big-name US market underperforms mid-cap and small-cap stocks and some of the foreign markets. Japan, England, Brazil, Mexico and Germany are among the more popular markets we follow closely in the United States. Is there merit in owning stocks in other markets to increase diversification? If so, how should an investor approach these markets? How can "Mrs. Donaldson," a working mother of three in Sioux City Iowa, diversify into these markets and not get screwed by Wall Street in the process?

Forget about actively managed mutual funds and rewarding Wall Street firms. We know that. In fact, when looking to invest in some of these other markets the expenses of mutual funds tend to be higher. There is apt to be more turnover and higher management fees compared to funds, which primarily invest in large capital domestic issues. Fund expense ratios of well over 2% are not uncommon and "Mrs. Donaldson" certainly doesn't need that.

Investors with little time on their hands may wish to consider investing in "MidCap Spiders" a long term unit trust designed to track the S & P MidCap 400 Index (as opposed to the S & P 500) again the benchmark for middle-capitalization stocks. The MidCap SPDR Trust is organized and traded just like "spider" or "diamonds." Only this time the trading symbol is MDY. The cost and turnover rate is very low as well because it's an indexed investment. Some familiar stocks contained in the Trust based upon review of the prospectus dated January 26, 1999 are: Borders Group, Sotheby's, Callaway Golf, Dole Foods, Harley-Davidson, NCR Corp., PaineWebber and Staples just to name a few. Chart 11, clearly indicates "MidCap Spiders" has not performed as well as SPDRs for the simple reason the greatest appreciation has occurred consistently, as of late, in the large cap. market. This may change and it might be beneficial for you and "Mrs. Donaldson" to be exposed to this market through the Trust.

CHART 11

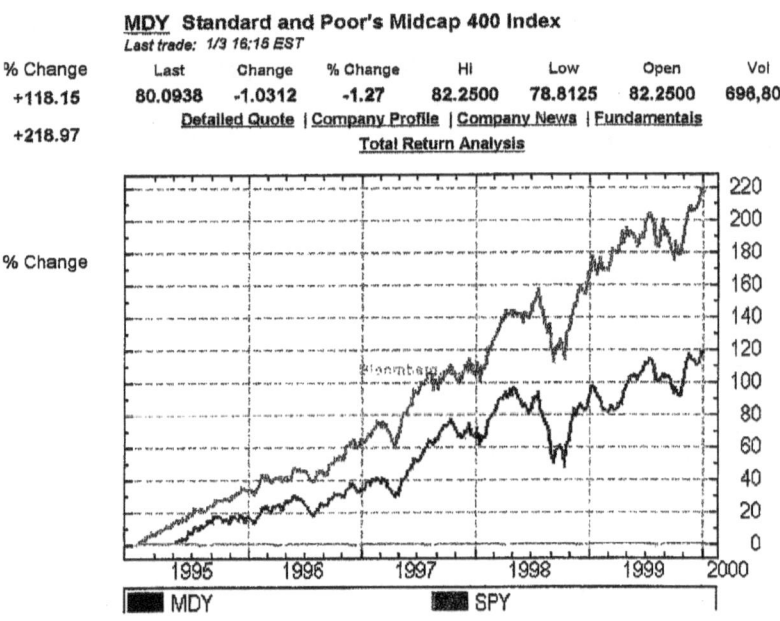

MDY Standard and Poor's Midcap 400 Index
Last trade: 1/3 16:16 EST

% Change	Last	Change	% Change	HI	Low	Open	Vol
+118.15	80.0938	-1.0312	-1.27	82.2500	78.8125	82.2500	696,80(

Detailed Quote | Company Profile | Company News | Fundamentals
Total Return Analysis

+218.97

Source: Reprinted, by permission of Bloomberg L.P.

Many new financial products and investment choices have been created to attract your investment dollar over the last ten years. This includes a plethora of choices to invest in overseas markets and coincides with the expansion of free-economies in Central and Eastern Europe, Asia and South America. However, investing in any foreign market just to be exposed to it, in order to further diversify your holdings, makes little sense if it is going to be a drag on your long-term after-tax returns. Just because the papers, magazines and news programs say investing overseas is a good thing -doesn't mean that it is or has been. Most foreign markets have vastly underperformed the S & P 500 for a great number of years. If we look at the graph below we can see how an index of Japanese, German and British stocks have fared over the last five years in relation to the S & P 500. The answer is not well.

CHART 12

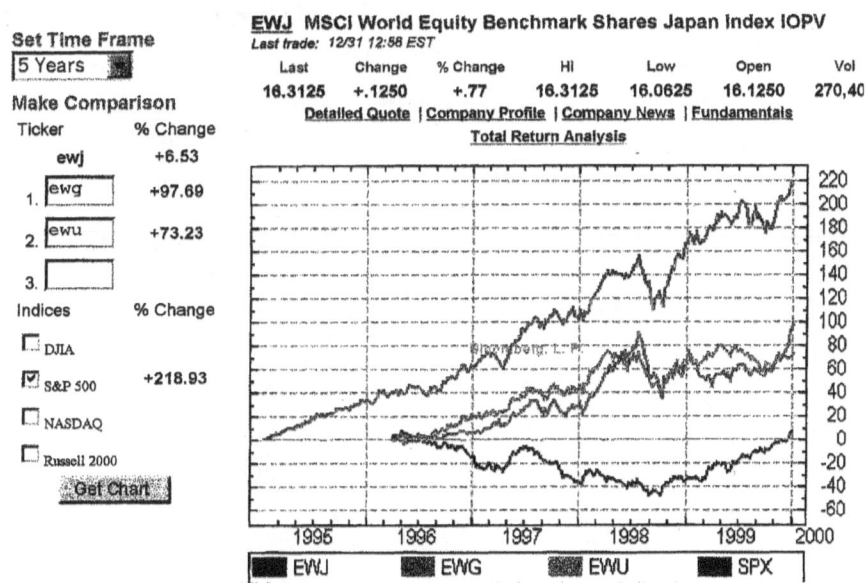

Source: Reprinted, by permission of Bloomberg L.P.

Okay, you've done some research and reading and you feel strongly that investing overseas is important. Instead of investing in a mutual fund that holds securities of foreign based companies I suggest looking at "webs" which does the same thing and seems to be a much healthier alternative. "Webs" are indexed investments and are more formally known as World Equity Benchmark Shares. "Webs" are AMEX traded and designed to track the performance of a particular Morgan Stanley Capital International index. At the end of October 1999, there were some fifty-four indices set up by Morgan Stanley to track performance in the developed world. There are many different "webs" from which to chose and invest. "Webs" give investors immediate exposure to other markets outside of the United States. These markets at some point outperform the S & P 500 or the Dow Jones Industrial Average. Chart 13 depicts the performance of the Japan, German and UK "webs" in relation to the S & P 500 over the last year ending December 1999.

CHART 13

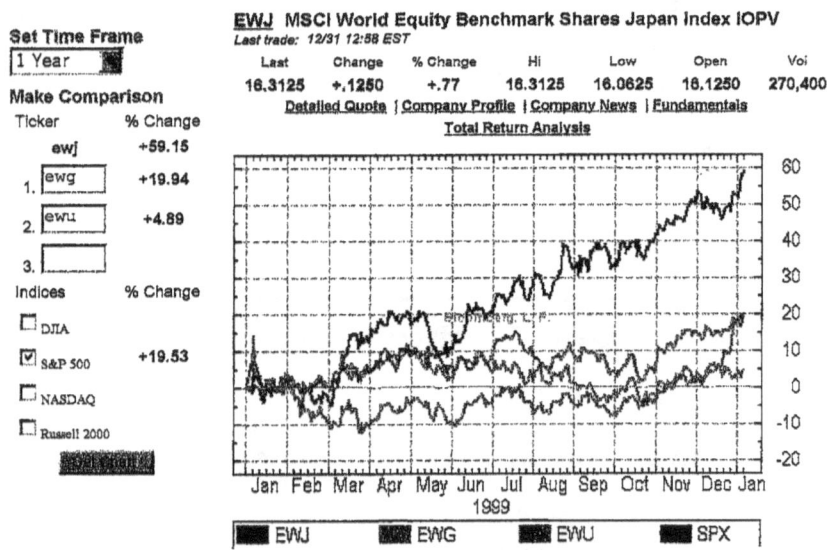

Source: Reprinted, by permission of Bloomberg L.P.

It can be judged from Chart 13 that even though the S & P 500 has greatly outperformed each of these indexed investments over the last five years or so, the Japan index has done much better than the S & P 500 over the last twelve months.

The answers to the questions: How long will the Japanese market outperform the S & P 500? When will the British and German markets take off and for how long? What will be the rate of return in each market in forthcoming years? No one knows of course. Does it make sense to invest overseas? Maybe. However, instead of giving your hard-earned dollar to the middleman to invest in foreign markets and get fleeced in the process pick out one or two "webs" or comparable index funds. Just as a domestic mutual fund may own General Electric, Microsoft and Intel in its portfolio, so too, is a German based fund likely to own companies such as: Adidas-Salomon, Daimler-Chrysler, Deutsche Telekom, Bayer, BASF, Lufthansa, SAP and Siemens. The point being, all of these well known firms are represented in Germany WEBS Index Series—so why pay a fund "operator" sometimes well over 2% annually to own these same stocks? You're naive, misinformed, misled or crazy if you do. I'm not suggesting you invest in any particular WEBS Index Series. It's your decision to make after proper thought and evaluation. However, as an alternative to a traditional mutual fund, I feel strongly you are likely to achieve superior results through indexing because costs are minimized.

Patricia Dunn, interviewed in the October 1999 issue *Money* magazine says in part, "....the S & P 500 reflects only one part of the market—large cap stocks. When small-caps start doing well, you'll want to be in either a broad market index or a small-cap index (or foreign index). They will have the same advantage over active managers as an S & P 500 index has over large-cap managers."[17] Indexing makes sense for investors trying to expose themselves to small-cap and foreign markets as well. Investors with little time or inclination to study investments should adopt the words "indexing." Find a few indexed investments most suitable for you. Maintain a regular investment plan and let your invested dollars work for you and compound over many years. If history means anything, you are much more likely to have a bigger pot of gold at the end of the rainbow by indexing than through mutual fund investing.

So, here's a course of action "Mrs. Donaldson" of Sioux City, Iowa can follow. She turns on her personal computer. She opens an online account by going to the web site of one of the do-it-yourself brokerage firms like AmeriTrade.com, E*Trade.com, or Schwab.com. She sets up the account in about ten minutes. She forgets about full service brokerage firms altogether because she wants to minimize her commissions and simply buy indexed investments. She doesn't need advice from a broker. "Mrs. Donaldson" has taken the time to research her intended index investments—be it "spiders" "diamonds" or one or two "webs" or any number of comparable index funds. She has developed a simple plan and certainly doesn't need a middleman to get in the way of the plan and detract from her wealth creation. She buys the indexed investments online and on her original $10,000 investment she pays $14.95 in commissions (which is the actual charge E*Trade quotes for a $10,000 investment in SPDRs). Fourteen dollars and ninety-five cents is a small price to pay for something she is intent on owning for many years. "Mrs. Donaldson" maintains the account and continues to closely follow her investment plan by placing money into the market regularly into the indexed investments. Even though "Mrs. Donaldson" is a working mother of three young children and only spends about twenty minutes each year on investing her hard-earned capital, she has created a very powerful and easy-to-manage portfolio. The great thing about it is "Mrs. Donaldson" is likely to beat most of the pros on Wall Street and their highly touted and publicized investment schemes. Her cash is not idly sitting around in some mutual fund. If she wants to keep cash on hand she can open a checking account and purchase a few certificates of deposit with her local bank. "Mrs. Donaldson" of Sioux

City has effectively whittled down the average annual costs of mutual fund ownership of 2.28% to next to nothing through indexing. In twenty-five years time she has amassed a small fortune by keeping the 2.28% in her pocket—away from the middleman.

Needless to say I believe in the simple logic offered through index investing. While I was at Morgan Stanley Dean Witter, I felt my clients would be better served in some of these investments. The problem was I couldn't make a living at the firm promoting them. At a full service firm like the one I was at a $10,000 investment in "spiders" would generate commissions of $150 or so. Whereas, the same $10,000 would generate about $575, or a 5.75% fee, if invested in a loaded mutual fund. Brokers who make a living on a commission basis tend to view mutual funds and indexed investments as one shot deals—meaning once the money is invested it's not likely to produce any meaningful commissions for a very long period time. In the mind of a broker it's "dead money." I used to think the money had wings and wouldn't come back my way for about thirty years. Therefore, if brokers are to choose between selling "spiders" or loaded mutual funds, most will chose the later. While I was at Morgan Stanley Dean Witter not one time did senior management ever express, promote or educate the brokers about the various indexed investments and how important they could be for clients. There was no point to because the firm had its own mutual funds and investment advisory services and that was how it made its money. So, if you currently deal with a full service broker and you haven't received a phone call from him or her lately suggesting you buy "spiders" or "Mid-Cap spiders" now you know why. The good news is that these investments are catching on and growing in popularity but with little thanks to the middleman on Wall Street.

PART 3

What You Probably Should Do

So far in this book we have discussed some of the things to avoid investing in and some of the things that hold much better prospects for investors. The big decision investors have with the investments discussed has been to select the "best" fund or the "best" index which will in turn hold many individual investments. After deciding on the fund or index, and when and how much to buy, the investor has basically nothing else to do. The performance of the investment(s) is driven by the decisions of the mutual fund "operator," the market and the index selection committee. As an investor you can put your mind at rest. You must live with the phrase, "and leave the driving to us" because the investment returns have nothing to do with you. The good news is you can concentrate your efforts in other areas of your life—like family, lowering your handicap, reading or photography. The bad news is don't ever expect your investment portfolio to do better than the market.

The only way for investors to beat the market over a long period of time is to commit a lot of time, effort and energy. You must believe in yourself first and foremost. You must acquire the knowledge and skills to do so. You must invest by yourself and trust your own instincts. You must not be afraid to make an investment decision and to buy with "conviction." You must forget about entrusting your money and any decision making that goes along with it to anyone but yourself. You must divorce yourself from the hype created by others in the market. To beat the market, it means avoiding "tips" from your best friend at work, the bartender, or the barber. It means possibly giving up your weekend golf game, parties, dates and family time to sit around home and read annual reports. It means improving your investment skills continually through reading, lectures and classes. If you are not able to make these self-sacrifices, then you are probably doing yourself a disservice and should probably follow a much simpler course and buy a few indexed investments. For those bold enough, the next part of the book is for you.

I believe the market can be outperformed over a lengthy period of time because others have done it. One such person that's done it is Warren Buffett, Chairman of Berkshire Hathaway, Inc. He has come as close as any one at perfecting the art of investing. Mr. Buffett has become the second wealthiest individual in the United States (second only to his buddy Bill Gates) through the increased appreciation of his approximate 478,000 shares of Berkshire Hathaway stock. Mr. Buffett's primary duty at the firm is to allocate capital, which he does by buying other companies for investment purposes. His investment strategies and actions have paid off handsomely. Chart 14, shows how superior Berkshire Hathaway stock has performed in relation to the S & P 500 over the last fifteen years or so.

CHART 14

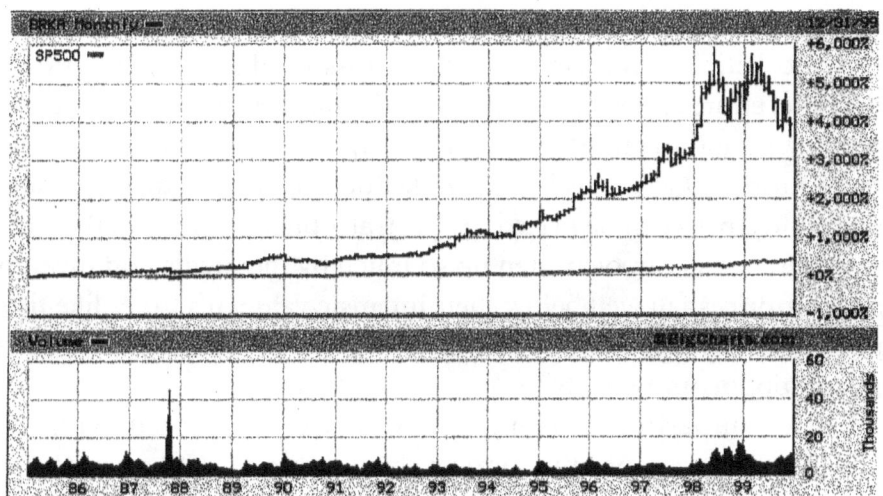

Source: Reprinted, by permission of BigCharts.com

If you were fortunate enough to have bought one share of Berkshire Hathaway stock in January 1985 at $1,275 and held it for fifteen years through 1999, you would have received an annualized rate of return of about 29%. By year-end 1999, your $1,275 investment would have grown to nearly $60,000. Conversely, a $1,275 investment in the S & P 500 would have grown to just shy of $13,500. Berkshire Hathaway stock, through Mr. Buffett's leadership, bettered the S & P 500 by about 12% over the last fifteen years.

Mr. Buffett's investment performance lends support that we should reject the "efficient market hypothesis" discussed earlier. He's proven with time, effort and energy expended, the market can be bettered over a lengthy period of time. Human greed and emotions run the market and because of that prices in the market do not always equate to value. As a result, stocks can be priced in the stratosphere relative to their true worth. Or, stocks can be beaten up so much by the media and investors that their prices fall well below their intrinsic value. It's times like these that afford the knowledgeable and astute investor (like Warren Buffett) a savory opportunity to strike.

But to outperform the market you are confronted with two problems: First, you need to locate a small group of stocks you feel are worth committing to and owning for a very long period of time. Second, is to know when to "pull the trigger" and to invest in each particular company. Your goal is to create a portfolio of five to eight companies over a period of time you believe in with conviction. The small portfolio becomes your arsenal to provide you with the highest after-tax return possible.

One of the first things to do is to find companies and industries you understand. The first rule is to trust your instincts and invest in what you know. Warren Buffett for example, doesn't have significant ownership in Microsoft or Intel (if any) because he doesn't fully understand the industry. He claims he doesn't know how it will evolve and because of that, he can't calculate earnings and cash flow in the future. To him, there is just too much uncertainty and too many changes occurring in technology to commit capital. Of course there are exceptions. I have a very close friend who has basically no idea what Cisco Systems does. As best as he can explain it, "If two or more computers need to talk to each other then Cisco handles it." Equipped with this in-depth knowledge, my friend was somehow lucky enough to have bought the stock five or six years ago. Cisco was recently cited by *Fortune* magazine to be the top stock of the last decade—far out surpassing the S & P 500.

The next important rule to follow is to invest in companies that are consistent. This means finding companies, which have demonstrated steady and increased earnings over a very long period of time (ten years minimum). Of the two companies indicated below, Occidental Petroleum and Coca-Cola, it's easy to see which holds more attraction to us, on this basis.

$ Earnings Per Share

	1998	1997	1996	1995	1994	1993	1992	1991	1990	1989
Occidental	.99	(1.43)	.73	1.31	(.36)	. 80	(1.97)	1.52	(5.82)	
Coca-Cola	1.43	1.67	1.40	1.18	.99	84	. 72	.61	.51	.43

Source: www.oxy.com (December 15, 1999)
              www.cocacola.com (December 15, 1999)

Consistency is vitally important because it makes the job of predicting future performance much easier. Mr. Buffett, too, strongly believes that the value of a business is simply determined by discounting the expected cash flows generated at a certain rate. The tough part is generating those cash flows and that's why it's so important to have some degree of consistency to begin with.

Companies should show consistency in more than earnings too. They should have strong and healthy balance sheets, which aren't tinkered with capital infusions. The reason being, if a company needs more money, it's usually because it's running out of what it's got. That's not a good thing to involve yourself in. A very healthy company doesn't need anybody's help because it can grow through internally generated funds. When companies raise funds by issuing more shares of stock, it dilutes the ownership for existing shareholders. So, when you pick up a Wall Street Journal next time and see all the notices about firms raising capital through their investment bankers—it's usually not in your best interest to take part.

The second important component to your overall return from stocks comes from dividends. Remember that historically about 30% of the market's return come by way of dividends. Companies, which have paid dividends consistently for many years and at increasing amounts, are very good to look at. Again examine the dividends paid to shareholders by Coca-Cola and Occidental.

	$ Dividends per Share									
	1998	1997	1996	1995	1994	1993	1992	1991	1990	1989
Occidental	1.00	1.00	1.00	1.00	1.00	1.00	1.00	1.00	2.50	2.50
Coca-Cola	.60	.56	.50	.44	.39	.34	.28	.24	.20	.17

Source: www.oxy.com (December 15, 1999)
www.cocacola.com (December 15, 1999)
www.sec.gov (December 15, 1999)

Yet another important concept to grasp, and which is rarely discussed with stock ownership, is the notion of return on cost. Let's say you purchased Coke in 1989 at $8 per share and received an annual dividend of $.17. The yield on the stock at the time was therefore 2.125%. Not bad, but certainly nothing to write home about. In fact, in comparison to a thirty-year treasury bond yielding near 9% in 1989 you were forfeiting quite a bit of return. So what happens a decade later? The

Treasury bond still pays 9%. The government hasn't felt obligated to give you one red cent more. But, your yield on cost of Coke stock has gone all the way up to 7.5% because you are now being paid $.60 on your $8 investment through dividend increases. The gap in yields slowly closes and the benefits of owning Coca-Cola becomes more apparent. By 1999, simply holding on to your Coke shares you are being paid in excess of 7.5% of cost. It's time for you to write home and tell the family because interest rates have fallen since 1989. As an investor in late 1999 you could buy a thirty-year Treasury bond yielding only a little more than 6%. What began as a modest yield in 1989 has really turned out to be quite an attractive one by 1999. Your decade ownership and patience has paid off handsomely by way of capital appreciation and increased dividends. A high yield on cost is a good thing for investors and is directly attributable to increased dividends. Of course this is a foreign concept to mutual fund "operators" because of the standard 85% turnover rate. Incidentally, an investment in Coke returned approximately 30% to investors for the decade ending 1998 compared to approximately 12% for the bond (which includes price appreciation).

Typically with long term ownership, return on cost goes up over time. The problem (if it is a problem) is as it does, it becomes tougher and tougher to sell stocks which have been marginal performers. From my own experience, I purchased Philip Morris about ten years ago when its yield was about 3%. It wasn't even a "dog" at the time. By 1999 my yield on cost had risen in excess of 10%. I find it hard to sell a stock like that especially when I'll be forced to pay about one-third of my gains to Uncle Sam and to the State. If I did sell, I'd be left with two-thirds of the money I have now and I couldn't get close to a reinvestment rate of 10%. Sticking with Philip Morris stock, which has been going through a lengthy dry spell, is not so bad when you are being paid 10% for your patience. So, when sizing up companies to invest in, look to see if the dividends have been increasing consistently over time.

Another important element, which seems to be found in many great companies, is the consistency in how the firm operates and what it does. It's probably a good idea to stay away from companies which are undergoing drastic management changes, product changes (or new widget introductions), as well as companies which are growing through zealous buying sprees. Take Coke for example. The firm makes its money primarily doing one thing quite well and that is selling sugar water. It's been doing so for about one hundred years. In the past, many firms have tried entering unrelated businesses—only to fail miserably at it. Coca-Cola in the 1970's diversified into owning a few shrimp farms (Bubba Gump would be proud) and a winery. These were found to be low margin businesses and were later sold by the next chief executive officer. Take Occidental Petroleum for example, which for years owned the largest beef company in Iowa, only to later sell it so the company could "concentrate on its core business." Many scenarios like this exist in corporate America where an acquiring company's first mistake was acquiring. I believe the best companies stick with what they know how to do well and don't change their game plan. When you read in the *Wall Street Journal*, "Management has decided to divest itself of XYZ and to concentrate on its core business of ABC," be cautious about investing. This usually means a part of the company is not working out well and is not profitable. Comments like these may point to a company in search of its own identity and purpose with no real direction and a host underlying problems. Be wary when you read, "Mr. Smith, Chairman and CEO for about two years and several of his underlings have decided to retire to pursue "other interests." These statements can point towards a company in upheaval with internal politics and fighting. It's not a place to tie up capital. When you invest in a company look for management that's been in tact for many years with a proven track record. Take General Electric for example, John "Jack" Welch, Jr., the current Chairman & CEO, has been with the firm in a senior capacity for over twenty years.

Finally be wary when you read in the Journal, " The firm has recently completed its sixth multi-billion dollar acquisition in the last four years." This points to leaders of a company that have testosterone levels much too high for their own good —whereby they need to feed their egos through corporate domination. Many times companies pay too much to acquire other firms. As a result, the overpayment hurts the acquiring company. When a bidding war ensues for a company it's usually the firm which agrees to pay the most wins the battle. When the dust finally settles, many times the firm which won the battle actually loses the war because it paid too much to begin with (think back to the 1980's with all the high priced leveraged buyouts). Stay away from companies, which exhibit a lot of growth through acquisition. These actions can hurt shareholders terribly. Look for companies, which expand internally—by gaining current market share in existing markets and in penetrating new ones.

When companies are consistent in all areas of their businesses, it makes the job of prediction so much easier and precise for the investor. And, **the more certain you can become of what the future holds for a particular company, the better investment decision you are likely to make.**

Another important trait great companies tend to exhibit is a demonstrated high return on equity while at the same time utilizing little if any debt. Return on equity is the relationship of profit achieved to equity. Return on equity can be thought of in terms of the money you get back each year from your down payment used to purchase a four-unit apartment building. The rent you receive minus all the operating expenses (like maintenance, utilities, insurance and taxes) and mortgage payments hopefully provides you with something left over. Whatever that amount is, divided by the amount of money you put down to buy the property is your return on equity. Stocks are viewed in a similar fashion. Return on equity is measured by the equation of Net Income / Stockholder's Equity and it is one of the most important relationships to judge an investment. A very strong company will have a very high and consistent ratio. It's better to achieve this high percentage without the use of much debt (or borrowed money). As a rule of thumb, **search for companies which have displayed a consistent return on equity of at least 18% and which have a total debt to total asset ratio under 50%.**

Comparing Coca-Cola to Occidental Petroleum we can easily judge which one meets the above standard.

Return on Equity %

	1998	1997	1996	1995	1994	1993
Occidental	10.8	(11.1)	11.2	9.0	(5.0)	7.1
Coca-Cola	45.1	61.6	60.8	56.4	52.1	51.8

Total Debt to Total Asset %

	1998	1997	1996	1995	1994	1993
Occidental	77.9	71.9	65.7	69.8	71	80.7
Coca-Cola	26.9	23	28	27.1	25.3	25.8

Source:www.oxy.com (December 15, 1999)
      www.cocacola.com (December 15, 1999)
      www.sec.gov (December 15, 1999)

Coca-Cola has an extremely high and consistent return on equity. Occidental does not. Coke has further achieved its fine performance with little debt on its balance sheet. Occidental on the other hand is highly leveraged. It may come as no surprise that Coke provided about a 30% annualized return to shareholders for the previous ten years through 1998, while Occidental could only muster a shade over 2.5%. It's no wonder stockholders have been complaining to management at

Occidental—especially when the chief executive officer has been compensated more than $1 million annually during this time. Investors would have been better off having their funds in an interest bearing checking account.

As a general rule you should probably stay away from capital intensive companies. These are firms, which, in order to continue to produce or manufacture their widgets, need to spend a lot of money to build, maintain and upgrade facilities. These companies tend to be asset rich and, because of that, tend to have low rates of return on assets. This important financial ratio is judged by taking Net Income/ Total Assets. Great companies tend to have high rates of return on assets (relative to companies in its peer group) in addition to returns on equity. For example, Microsoft's ROA was 26.2% and Intel's was 20.1% in the last fiscal year as www.etrade.com indicated at year-end 1999. These are high percentages in comparison to Occidental which reported a 2.1% ROA or Union Carbide which reported a 5.7% ratio. Related to real estate, return on assets can be likened to owning a ten-unit apartment building, which provides the same net income as one containing one hundred units. Companies that have a lot of assets tied up in plant, property and equipment (or fixed assets) tend to have low profit margins, low returns on assets and low returns on equity. Put another way—unless you are looking at a banking concern (which primarily makes a spread off borrowed funds), **great companies tend to make a lot of money not owning and not owing very much.** Take an oil company for example. Just think how much an oil-drilling platform may cost to build and maintain in the Bering Sea? Or an automobile company that decides to build a new 1,000,000 square foot assembly plant in small town USA? Unless, it's a dramatically different widget (which the latest Chevy or oil from Alaska isn't) these expenses tend not to alter the performance of the company significantly or help a shareholder's attempt at early retirement.

Instead, look for companies, which produce the same widget year after year without high infrastructure costs. Don't you think Coca-Cola (a soft drink company), Wrigley & Company (a chewing gum company) or even Morgan Stanley Dean Witter (an investment company) have relatively fewer assets tied up long term to produce its widget than say an oil or chemical company? The answer doesn't require much thought. All three of these companies are highly efficient, profitable, and have been very kind to shareowners compared to others (like Occidental). Great companies are like greyhound dogs—efficient with not a lot of wasted fat surrounding them.

Time and time again people say invest in companies with "good management." This is true, but what does it mean? I've never heard the term clearly defined by any of Harvard's best on television. In my opinion, good management sets a clear course for the company in the future. They have a vision of how and where it will profitably grow. In order to accomplish that task, good management effectively utilizes the capital at its disposal and greatly increases shareholder wealth in the process. We measure the performance of management by looking at the return on equity, the earnings per share growth, and the profit margins and of course the value of the stock.

There are plenty of good companies around that meet the various financial tests outlined as potential investments. Occidental Petroleum, however is not one of them. Coke is, and maybe you can see why Warren Buffett became so interested in it and now owns 200,000,000 shares.

The first step in creating your simple portfolio must be to locate those companies, which excite you, based on your sphere of knowledge, your research and analysis. You may only find one company once in a while that meets your criteria for owning. That's fine—**holding a small portfolio of stocks is your best method to beat the market.** Too much diversification is a prescription for mediocrity and you certainly don't want that. In other words, in order to have a snowball's chance in hell of beating the market year after year, you are going to need to limit the number of stocks you own.

The second important step to assembling your portfolio is to value the stock(s) you've earmarked for ownership. Valuing stocks is an imperfect science. There is no one right way to do it. One method is to do a complex discounted cash flow analysis. That's what you learn how to do in a finance class in business school. A detailed discounted cash flow can take months to prepare and the person preparing it can flaw it. When I was in business school, I noticed that two people rarely, if ever, came up with the same valuation for a stock. Another, and easier way to value a particular stock is to rely on its past earnings history. Dig a little and you can determine a company's prior earnings per share growth rate (say 8%, 15% or 30%). The growth rate you come up with then becomes the price earnings multiple (or commonly known as the PE ratio, found daily in newspapers) you use to "trigger" your buy decision. For example, the earnings growth rate of Coca-Cola over the last ten fiscal years through 1998 has been about 12.75% (earnings per share rising from $.43 in 1989 to $1.43 by 1998), for Intel about 29.5% (EPS was $.13 in 1989 rising to $1.73 by 1998) and finally for drug giant Merck about 13% (EPS rising from $.625 in 1989 to $2.150 by 1998). Applying this logic, it means you'll agree to pay no more than either 12.75, 29.5 or 13 times earnings to own these fine companies. In other words, for every $1 of earnings at Coke you'll pay $12.75 to own it; for every $1 of earnings at Intel you'll pay $29.50 to own it; and finally at Merck you'll pay $13 for every $1 of earnings. You've assigned a buy price. Next, you compare the current price of the stock and its price earnings ratio to the price you'll pay given the multiple you've derived. If the price is at or below your estimate of value—you simply place an order and buy the stock. This approach to stock valuation is completely valid unless of course you have some detailed knowledge that leads you to believe that growth will occur faster or slower at a particular company. You might just harbor a strong conviction that Coca-Cola is likely to double its growth rate (to 25.5%) in the future because it's penetrating new markets (you may believe Coke will become the number #1 beverage in China by 2010 surpassing tea), cutting costs or developing exciting new products. If so, using the historic growth rate of Coke doesn't do you much good. In the market, companies do (or should) trade on the basis of projected earnings growth and I believe the past is usually the best indication of future performance. Warren Buffett states it this way in an interview with *Fortune* magazine in late 1999: " The inescapable fact is that the value of an asset, whatever its character, cannot over the long term grow faster than its earnings do."[18]

If a company, no matter how attractive it is, is trading at a price earnings ratio higher than the earnings per share growth rate calculated, I won't buy the stock. One thing I simply don't understand today are the valuations placed by the market on many technology and Internet related companies. Prices have been bid up to levels in many cases, which have no relation to past, present or even the wildest projections for future earnings growth. Take Cisco Systems for example. Many people have become wealthy owning it over the last five to ten years (I'm not one of them). The earnings for the company over the last four quarters has been about $.60, up about 30% from the prior year, and somehow it's trading at a PE ratio close to 170 or $102 per share. Its earnings growth rate is nowhere near 170%. It's much closer to the 30% figure—I guarantee that. A PE ratio of that figure implies the market believes earnings per share will more than double in years to come. No large company has ever experienced that rate in EPS growth for any measurable length of time. Or look at Ebay, which earned $.06 per share over the last four quarters, more than in any prior period, yet it's selling at about $175 per share at an astronomical PE ratio. Finally, look at Amazon.com which has no net earnings and trades at about $85 per share. There has been a lot of speculative zeal running through the market in late 1990's. Many Internet related stocks have been trading at multiples consistently high during the decade. As long as the market continues to place such high multiples on these stocks, investors will not get hurt. Look at Cisco again, let's say the earnings go up next year 25% to $.75. If the market still places a PE ratio on the stock of 170, the stock will rise to about $127 per share. The investor's shares grow in value 25% for the year from $102 to $127. But, I believe at some point there will be a day of reckoning for those companies (like Cisco) which are priced in the stratosphere and well above any possibly attained or sustained rate of growth. I'm certainly not alone in my thinking. John Kenneth Galbraith, one of the great economists of the twentieth century, comments in the *Los Angeles Times* on December 12, 1999: "We are now experiencing a classic manifestation of the speculative bubble. The only thing I can say is the speculative bubble always comes to an end—and never in a pleasant or peaceful way."[19] The risk of buying into these high priced companies is very real for investors. At some point the market is going to realize the relationship between earnings growth and market price. The only questions that remain are just when will this happen—when will the market begin to re-price these overvalued securities and how severe will the correction be. There is no reason why Cisco shouldn't be trading at $46 per share commanding a PE ratio of 82. Conventional wisdom would still tell us it's overpriced even at half its current price. Investing or putting your money into companies, whose valuations defy gravity, can be likened to a giant pyramid scheme—where those last in lose.

As an investor you must understand the market can act irrationally. Just as many Internet stocks have become overvalued in the market (represented by price earnings ratios far exceeding growth rates), so too, does the market undervalue stocks. It's just very hard to find undervalued securities today because, as the Dow has been reaching new highs, the PE ratio of the market has expanded as well, to about twenty-four times earnings. In a nutshell, the PE ratio of the market today greatly exceeds the growth rates of most companies and that's why it's so hard to find good bargains. That's not always the case though. For example, Intel is currently trading at about thirty-five times earnings and above its EPS growth rate the last ten years of 29.5% or so. But, I remember in June 1994 when you could have bought Intel while it was trading at eleven times earnings because the market overreacted to a flawed chip introduced by the company. Or take Fannie Mae, which currently trades at a PE ratio of about nineteen today and fairly close to its historic ten-year growth rate. But, I remember in late 1994, Fannie Mae was trading at only nine times earnings as investors drove bank and other financially related stocks down during a year of interest rate escalations by the Fed. I remember Merck, which now trades at a multiple above thirty, trading at about fifteen times earnings in 1993 because of the market's overreaction to the newly elected President's proposed health care reform. I remember when the "mad cow" disease in Great Britain kept the price of McDonald's stock down throughout most of 1995. When Warren Buffett made a sizable investment in Coca-Cola in 1988, the stock was trading near a price earnings ratio of fifteen. Today, Coca-Cola stock is trading at about fifty-five times earnings and well above its earnings per share growth rate. The point is the market is likely to afford you bargains again in some of those "gems" you've located and researched—be it Intel, General Electric or XYZ Company. As an investor you must be patient for buying opportunities to present themselves in the stocks you want to own. The bigger the discount in the market to the intrinsic value you place on the stock the better for you.

The third and final key to wealth creation, although it may seem obvious, is to buy a lot of stock when you buy it. In other words when you see a great buying opportunity—strike with vengeance; get greedy and don't pussyfoot around. If you believe in a stock, you might as well own as much as possible. A $100 investment compounding at 20% a year for twenty years won't make you rich but one of sizable magnitude will. The compounding effect on your invested dollar is very real and it can help alter the course of your life in years to come. For every $10,000 you invest today, you'll have an additional $70,000 in pretax dollars in twenty years if you achieve just the average return of the market of 11%. But, with research, time, effort and patience I believe you can do better than the market in years to come. If the market continues to march along at about a 18% clip (as it has over the last ten years) and you are able to better it by 2%, and you are able to sock away ten, twenty or thirty thousand dollars or more, your retirement years might just be everything you envisioned. A 20% pre tax return will provide you with about $373,000 in twenty years for every $10,000 investment you make. If owning a lot of just a few stocks has been Warren Buffett's pattern to create billions, it might as well become yours to create a few million.

One last thing. Once you've purchased your five to eight "gem" stocks hold them and put them away and don't tinker with them. Sometimes selling is a necessary evil—like paying for medical emergencies, your children's college education, your daughter's wedding or son's bar mitzvah. But, outside of these or a few other reasons—hold your selected stocks. Selling only creates commissions for your broker and probable capital gains tax to the state and Uncle Sam. If you sell, and are intending to reinvest, then you are starting the process over again of what to do with your uninvested funds. You are also likely to have less capital to invest than you had prior to the sale because of the hand of the taxman. Here's an example of the buy and hold strategy at its best: My father is now seventy years old and he has regularly invested in the stock market throughout his life. In 1950, just after he graduated college, he bought one hundred shares of Pitney Bowes stock, costing $1,771. He's held the stock for about fifty years and never added to or sold any of his shares. At the end of 1999, he owned 10,464 shares of the stock with an approximate market value of $425,000. That's not all. He's also received quarterly dividends since the time of his purchase. His quarterly dividend now amounts to $2,668, which is 150% of his original $1,771 investment in 1950. His annual income is $10,672 on the one hundred-share investment. His return on cost is about 600%

because of dividend increases throughout the years. Now that's an "investment!" No bond and no mutual fund performs like that.

You can tell by now I wasn't the leading commissioned securities salesperson in the business. My buy and hold strategy to create wealth wasn't a great method to create fees for the firm or income for myself. Yet, this is the best approach, I'm convinced, for investors to follow. An inherent contradiction existed for me, which I simply couldn't digest.

Fayez Sarofim, one of the great investors in this century and reportedly to be worth $1.5 billion was recently interviewed in the October 1999 issue of *Money* magazine. The article states in part, "Sarafim's success stems largely from his gift for picking great growth stocks—from Wal-Mart to GE, Gillette to Merck. Equally important, though, he's had the mental strength to hang on to his favorites for years, while lesser investors jump in and out on every quarterly earnings report. "Basically, everybody is a short-term investor today," he says, with an air of quiet amusement. What quality sets him apart? "Patience."" Later in the interview Mr. Sarofim claims, " The biggest mistake is selling your winners. You should hold on to the ones that have done well and sell the others. It's the exact opposite of what most people do." The interview concludes when he is asked, "to recount another humbling mistake. In the 1950s, he says, he sold a painting by Childe Hassam for $25,000; he'd bought it for $1,100, and he was delighted with his profit. "Now," he chuckles, "it would be worth $400,000." The lesson? "Never sell.""[20]

In order to create substantial wealth in years to come it's best to avoid putting a nickel into any actively managed mutual fund. The management fees, expenses, high turnover rates, cash balances and commissions, we have seen, fleeces you and unnecessarily so. You don't need to line the pockets of the middlemen on Wall Street at your expense. You deserve better. Don't look at other gimmicks Wall Street has created to siphon your money either—like hiring a "money manager" or investing in certain unit investment trusts. We have seen a much more productive way to invest is to open an on-line account and invest in indexed investments. You are likely to keep more money in your pocket, which will grow for you. It's time for more of us to turn our Backs on Wall Street. We should thank them though for educating us about the merits of investing and retirement planning. We should thank them because more people have invested in the market and converted their 4% savings accounts to equity ownership. But, that is about the extent of it. You can do much better for yourself in years to come without Wall Street's interference. If you are bold enough find the stocks yourself and create a small portfolio. Tuck them away and let long-term equity ownership work for you. I can't guarantee what the market will do in the next ten, twenty or thirty years. But I can guarantee you a few things:

1. Investing today is paramount to your financial well-being later in life.
2. In 275 million years from now none of what's been discussed here will really matter.
3. Mel Gibson and Goldie Hawn won't be starring in a major motion picture adopted from this writing.

Appendix A

Stocks in the Dow Jones Industrial Average as of December 31, 1999:

Alcoa	American Express
AT & T	Boeing
Caterpillar	Citigroup
Coca-Cola	Disney
DuPont	Eastman Kodak
Exxon Mobil	General Electric
General Motors	Hewlett-Packard
Home Depot	Honeywell
Intel	IBM
International Paper	Johnson & Johnson
McDonald's Corp.	Merck
Microsoft	MMM
J.P. Morgan	Philip Morris
Procter & Gamble	SBC Communications
United Technologies	Wal-Mart

Notes

1. Michael Sivy and Brian P. Murphy, "How to Focus your Investing," *Money*, November 1999, 107.

2. Bill Barker, "The Performance of Mutual Funds," Available: http://search.fool.com/school/mutualfunds/performance/record. html (December 15, 1999).

3. Bill Barker, "Turnover and Cash Reserves," Available: http://search.fool.com/school/mutualfunds/costs/turnover. html (December 15, 1999).

4. Ibid.

5. Bill Barker, "Loads," Available: http://search.fool.com/school/mutualfunds/costs/loads.html (December 15, 1999).

6. Bill Barker, "Turnover and Cash Reserves," Available: http://search.fool.com/school/mutualfunds/costs/turnover.html (December 15, 1999).

7. Ibid.

8. Suzanne Woolley, Pablo Galarza and William Green, "The Ultimate Investment Club," *Money*, October 1999, 83.

9. Randy Befumo, "A Lesson in Tax Efficiency," Available: http://search.fool.com/school/mutualfunds/costs/efficiency.html (December 20, 1999).

10. *Morningstar Mutual Funds*, 1999 ed.,s.v. "Resource Guide."

11. *The Investment Company Act of 1940*, Available:
http://www.law.uc.edu/CCL/InCoAct/sec12.html (December 20,
1999).

12. Bill Barker, "Expense Ratios," Available:
http://search.fool.com/school/mutualfunds/costs/ratios.html
(December 20, 1999).

13. David Harrell, "Fund of Funds: The Good, the Bad, and the Ugly,"
Available:
http://news.morningstar.com/news/MS/Funds101/fundsoffunds.ht
ml (December 15, 1999).

14. John J. Mack and Philip J. Purcell, *Morgan Stanley Dean Witter
Annual Report 1998*, 9.

15. Available: http://www300.fidelity.com/about/world/manage.html
(December 15, 1999).

16. Suzanne Woolley, Pablo Galarza and William Green, "The Ultimate
Investment Club," *Money*, October 1999, 90.

17. Ibid.

18. Carol Loomis, "Mr. Buffett on the Stock Market," *Fortune*, 22
November 1999, 214.

19. Elizabeth Mehren, "John Kenneth Galbraith—A Liberal Eminence
Weighs the Economy of Compassion," *Los Angeles Times*, 12
December 1999, sec. M.

20. Suzanne Woolley, Pablo Galarza and William Green, "The Ultimate
Investment Club," *Money*, October 1999, 96.

About the Author

Ted Lux, is a well-known real estate and financial consultant in Los Angeles, CA and former Account Executive at Morgan Stanley Dean Witter. Mr. Lux is a resident of Pacific Palisades, CA and earned his BA degree from U.C.L.A and his MBA in finance from the University of Denver. Mr. Lux is originally from Shaker Hts, Ohio and remains an avid Cleveland Indians fan. To contact Mr. Lux please email him at edlux@yahoo.com